# GRAPHING AND INTERPRETING DATA

**GLOBE FEARON EDUCATIONAL PUBLISHER**
**A Division of Simon & Schuster**
Upper Saddle River, New Jersey

**Executive Editor:** Barbara Levadi
**Editors:** Bernice Golden, Lynn Kloss, Bob McIlwaine, Kirsten Richert
**Production Manager:** Penny Gibson
**Production Editor:** Walt Niedner
**Interior Design:** The Wheetley Company
**Electronic Page Production:** Curriculum Concepts
**Cover Design:** Pat Smythe

Printed in the United States of America 1 2 3 4 5 6 7 8 9 10 99 98 97 96

ISBN 0-8359-1563-8

**GLOBE FEARON EDUCATIONAL PUBLISHER**
**A Division of Simon & Schuster**
Upper Saddle River, New Jersey

# CONTENTS

bargraph— change of time

# TO THE STUDENT

*Access to Math* is a series of 15 books designed to help you learn new skills and practice these skills in mathematics. You'll learn the steps necessary to solve a range of mathematical problems.

**LESSONS HAVE THE FOLLOWING FEATURES:**

❖ Lessons are easy to use. Many begin with a sample problem from a real-life experience. After the sample problem is introduced, you are taught step-by-step how to find the answer. Examples show you how to use your skills.

❖ The *Guided Practice* section demonstrates how to solve a problem similar to the sample problem. Answers are given in the first part of the problem to help you find the final answer.

❖ The *Exercises* section gives you the opportunity to practice the skill presented in the lesson.

❖ The *Application* section applies the math skill in a practical or real-life situation. You will learn how to put your knowledge into action by using manipulatives and calculators, and by working problems through with a partner or a group.

Each book ends with *Cumulative Reviews*. These reviews will help you determine if you have learned the skills in the previous lessons. The *Selected Answers* section at the end of each book lists answers to the odd-numbered exercises. Use the answers to check your work.

Working carefully through the exercises in this book will help you understand and appreciate math in your daily life. You'll also gain more confidence in your math skills.

# INTERPRETING DATA FROM A TABLE

## Vocabulary

**data:** facts, measurements, and other information

**table:** an organized display of information

## Reminder

Rows run across. Columns run up and down.

Monique is planning to drive from her home in Atlanta to visit her sister in Chicago. How many miles will she drive?

### Distance Between U.S. Cities in Miles

|  | Atlanta | Chicago | Dallas | New York | Seattle |
|---|---|---|---|---|---|
| Atlanta |  | 674 | 795 | 841 | 2,618 |
| Chicago | 674 |  | 917 | 802 | 2,013 |
| Dallas | 795 | 917 |  | 1,552 | 2,078 |
| New York | 841 | 802 | 1,552 |  | 2,815 |
| Seattle | 2,618 | 2,013 | 2,078 | 2,815 |  |

The **table** above organizes road mileage **data.** You can use it to find the distance between different cities.

What is the distance between Atlanta and Chicago?

Atlanta ⟶ 674

*Find Atlanta on the left. Move across to the column labeled Chicago.*

The distance between Atlanta and Chicago is 674 miles.

Is Seattle nearer to Atlanta or New York?

Find Seattle on the left of the table. From Seattle to Atlanta is 2,618 miles and from Seattle to New York is 2,815 miles. Seattle is nearer to Atlanta.

## Guided Practice

1. What is the distance between Seattle and Dallas?

   **a.** Seattle is in the _____ row.

   **b.** Dallas is in the _____ column.

   **c.** The distance is _____ miles.

2. Which cities are farther than 1,000 miles from Chicago?

   **a.** Chicago is in the _____ row.

   **b.** The only city in the second row that is farther

   than 1,000 miles is _____

Use the table to answer the questions.

**Weekly Sit-Up Record**

|  | Monday | Tuesday | Wednesday | Thursday | Friday |
|---|---|---|---|---|---|
| **Peg** | 20 | 23 | 26 | 30 | 33 |
| **Anton** | 24 | 24 | 24 | 24 | 20 |
| **Sheray** | 40 | 10 | 56 | 24 | 33 |

**3.** On Wednesday, how many sit-ups did:

**a.** Anton do? _____

**b.** Peg do? _____

**c.** Sheray do? _____

**4.** Who did the most sit-ups on:

**a.** Monday?  **b.** Tuesday?  **c.** Thursday?

_____  _____  _____

**5.** On which day of the week was the total of sit-ups for all three students the greatest? The least? _____

**6.** Which student did the most sit-ups over the entire week? How many sit-ups did he or she do? _____

## Application

**7.** You can use the table to spot patterns, called trends, in the information. For example, which students showed improvement over the week? Which students didn't show improvement? Explain your answer.

_____

_____

_____

**8.** What other trends do you notice?

_____

_____

# CONSTRUCTING A TABLE

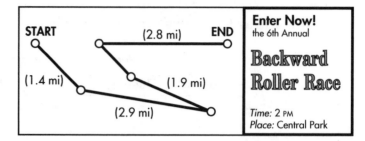

Every April 1, the city sponsors the Backward Roller Race. Skaters must skate backwards along a 10-mile race course. The race course has five sections, or legs. The distance for one of the legs was left off the map. What is its length?

To organize the information in a clearer way, use the map to make a table showing the length of each leg. First list each leg across the top of the table.

Then fill in the length of each leg.

| Leg | 1 | 2 | 3 | 4 | 5 |
|---|---|---|---|---|---|
| Length (miles) | 1.4 | 2.9 | 1.9 | ? | 2.8 |

You don't know how long leg 4 is, but you can figure it out. Add up all the other legs:

$$1.4 + 2.9 + 1.9 + 2.8 = 9.0 \ miles$$

Subtract this amount from 10 miles, the total distance of the course:

$$10.0 \ miles - 9.0 \ miles = 1.0 \ mile$$

Now you can complete the table.

| Leg | 1 | 2 | 3 | 4 | 5 |
|---|---|---|---|---|---|
| Length (miles) | 1.4 | 2.9 | 1.9 | ? | 2.8 |

## Guided Practice

1. Complete the table on page 5 to show the total distance skated at the end of each leg. Use the map or the table above.

   a. Write the lengths of leg 1 and leg 2. _____

   b. Find the sum of these legs. _____

   c. Fill in the sum for leg 2 on the table.

   d. Now find and fill in the sum for leg 3 on the table.

| Leg | 1 | 2 | 3 | 4 | 5 |
|---|---|---|---|---|---|
| Total Distance Skated | 1.4 | | | 7.2 | 10.0 |

Four fishing boats went out on Thursday. The size of their catch is shown in the picture.

2. Use the data to complete the table.

| Boat number | 1 | 2 | 3 | 4 |
|---|---|---|---|---|
| Boat name | King Lou | | | |
| Catch | | | | |

3. Make a second table. This time, list the boats in order, from biggest catch to smallest catch.

| Boat number | | | | |
|---|---|---|---|---|
| Boat name | | | | |
| Catch | | | | |

4. Collect data to make your own table. Interview five students in your class. Find out how many minutes they spend studying each week for the class and how they feel about school. Display your data in table form. Then analyze your data. Do students who like school seem to spend more time studying? Explain your answer.

# INTERPRETING A BAR GRAPH

## Vocabulary

**bar graph:** graph that uses bars to represent amounts

**horizontal axis:** runs across the top or bottom of a graph

**vertical axis:** runs up and down the left side of a graph

**scale:** a series of marks at known intervals on a line for the purpose of measuring

People use bar graphs so information can be quickly compared. About how many more Native Americans live in Los Angeles than in San Francisco?

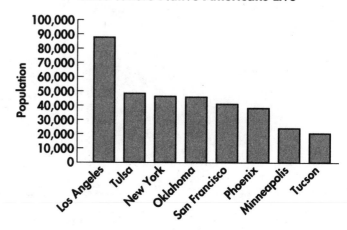

This **bar graph** shows the cities with the largest Native American populations. Each bar represents how many Native Americans live in each of the cities. The names of those cities are shown on the **horizontal axis**.

Look at the **scale** on the **vertical axis**. To estimate populations, line up the top of each bar with the scale.

Estimate: 87,000.                    Estimate: 41,000

This close up shows where the cities line up.

$$
\begin{array}{r}
87,000 \\
-\ 41,000 \\
\hline
46,000
\end{array}
$$

About 46,000 more Native Americans live in Los Angeles than in San Francisco.

## Guided Practice

1. About how many more Native Americans live in Phoenix than in Tucson?

   **a.** The mark for Phoenix seems close to _____.

   **b.** The mark for Tucson seems close to _____.

   **c.** About _____ more Native Americans live in Phoenix.

Use the bar graph below to estimate the Native American population of these states:

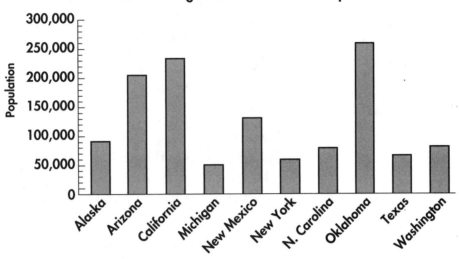

**States with Largest Native American Population**

**2.** California_____

**3.** Texas_____

**4.** New Mexico_____

**5.** Alaska_____

**6.** New York_____

**7.** Oklahoma_____

**8.** Which two states have about the same Native American population?

_____

## Application

You can get a lot of information from a graph just from a quick look. For example, just by looking at the first graph you can tell that Los Angeles has more Native Americans than any other American city.

**9.** Which states have less than half the population of Native Americans of Oklahoma?

_____

_____

**10.** Explain how you got your answer for problem 9.

_____

_____

# CONSTRUCTING A BAR GRAPH

## Reminder

The vertical axis runs up and down the left side of graph. The horizontal axis runs across the top or bottom of the graph.

The Broadcasting School took a survey of students' favorite television programs. How could you use this data to make a bar graph?

- *E.R.* was the favorite program of 28 students.
- *Seinfeld* was the favorite program of 72 students.
- *N.Y.P.D. Blue* was the favorite program of 49 students.

To construct a bar graph for this data, first make a vertical axis and a horizontal axis. Draw a scale on the vertical axis that represents the number of students in the survey. A scale from 0 to 80 is about right.

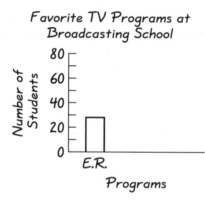

Draw a bar for *E.R.* first. Find 28 on the vertical scale. The top of the bar should line up with 28 students on the scale.

You might want to use a ruler or straight edge to line up each bar you draw.

Once the graph has been set up, label each bar showing the name of the television program. Then label the axes and write a title for the graph. The title should fully explain the information that is shown on the graph.

## Guided Practice

1. Draw a bar on the graph above for *Seinfeld*.

   **a.** How many people liked *Seinfeld* best? _____

   **b.** Line up this number on the graph.

   **c.** Draw a bar and label it *Seinfeld*.

2. Draw a bar for *N.Y.P.D. Blue*.

   **a.** How many people liked *N.Y.P.D. Blue* best?

   _____

**b.** Line up this number on the graph.

**c.** Draw a bar and label it *N.Y.P.D. Blue.*

**3.** Each week, television audiences are measured using rating points. Use the information on the table to graph the rating point data on the bar graph below.

| Program | E.R. | N.Y.P.D. Blue | 60 Minutes | Seinfeld |
|---------|------|---------------|------------|----------|
| Rating Points | 20 | 16 | 18 | 21 |

**4.** Label the axes, and title the graph.

**Application**

**5.** Collect television watching data for yourself. Record how long you spend watching television each day on the table below. Make a bar graph of your data.

| Day | Mon. | Tues. | Wed. | Thur. | Fri. | Sat. | Sun. |
|-----|------|-------|------|-------|------|------|------|
| Hours | | | | | | | |

**6.** Analyze your bar graph. What trends or patterns do you see?

_____

_____

_____

# DOUBLE BAR GRAPHS

## Vocabulary

**double bar graph:** a bar graph that compares two groups of data

**key:** a symbol that explains information on a graph

A **double bar graph** is used to make several comparisons between two similar groups of data using side-by-side bars. The double bar graph below compares the contents of one serving of fruit loops to one serving of granola. How many more grams is the serving size for granola than for fruit loops?

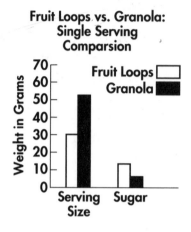

The **key** shows that the white bar represents fruit loops and the black bar represents granola.

You can see that the granola has a larger serving size than the fruit loops. The granola lines up near the number 50. Fruit loops line up near 30.

Granola weighs about 20 grams more than fruit loops per serving.

## Guided Practice

1. Read the graph to find out how many grams of sugar there are in each serving.

   **a.** Fruit loops has _____ grams of sugar.

   **b.** Granola has _____ grams of sugar.

   **c.** Fruit loops has _____ more grams of sugar per serving.

2. Graph this information to show how many fat grams are in fruit loops and granola per serving.

   • Fruit loops has about 1 gram of fat per serving.
   • Granola has about 6 grams of fat per serving.

   **a.** Draw each bar on the graph.

   **b.** Label the bars for fat on the horizontal axis.

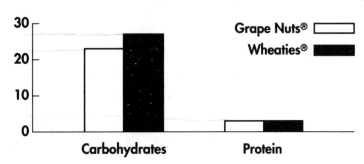

**Comparison: Grape Nuts® and Wheaties®**

**3.** Which cereal has more carbohydrates? _____

**4.** How many more grams of carbohydrates does it have? _____

**5.** How many grams of protein are in Grape Nuts®? In Wheaties®?

_____

## Application

**6.** Collect data to make your own double bar graph. Look at the nutrition labels for two foods that you like. Make a single serving comparison showing how many grams of sugar and fat they contain per serving. Graph the information on a double bar graph. Then label the axes and write a title.

**7.** Analyze your graph. Which food is more nutritious? Explain below.

_____

_____

_____

 **INTERPRETING A PICTOGRAPH**

**pictograph:** a graph that uses a picture of an object to represent a certain number of something

A **pictograph** uses picture symbols to help you understand data. In the pictograph below, each pizza symbol stands for 80 pizzas sold. How many pizzas does Pie in the Sky sell weekly?

**Average Weekly Pizza Sales**

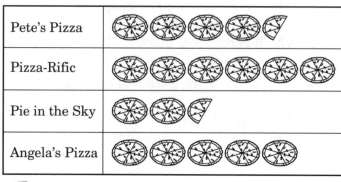

= 80 pizzas

Pie in the Sky's sales are shown as two and one half pizzas. The key below the pictograph shows that each picture of a whole pizza stands for 80 pizzas. Pie in the Sky's sales are represented by two and one half pizza symbols.

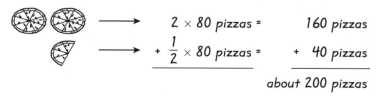

$$2 \times 80 \text{ pizzas} = 160 \text{ pizzas}$$
$$+ \frac{1}{2} \times 80 \text{ pizzas} = + 40 \text{ pizzas}$$
$$\text{about } 200 \text{ pizzas}$$

Pie in the Sky sells about 200 pizzas a week.

**Guided Practice**

**1.** How many pizzas does Pizza-Rific sell?

**a.** How many symbols are shown in the pictograph for Pizza-Rific? _____

**b.** Multiply whole symbols by 80. Multiply half-symbols by 40.

**c.** Add the two numbers together. Pizza-Rific sells _____ pizzas.

**2.** Write the pizza restaurant that fits each category. Who:

**a.** sells the most pizzas? _____

**b.** sells the fewest pizzas? _____

**c.** sells about 80 pizzas fewer than Pizza-Rific?

_____

---

**Weekly Sales: Angela's Pizza**

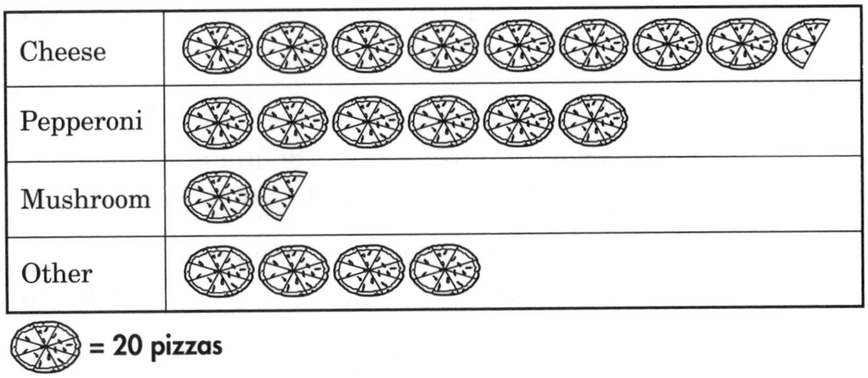

| Cheese | |
|---|---|
| Pepperoni | |
| Mushroom | |
| Other | |

= 20 pizzas

**Write which kind of pizza fits each category.**

**3.** Most popular pizza: _____

**4.** Least popular pizza: _____

**5.** Second-most popular pizza: _____

**About how many of each kind of pizza did Angela's sell?**

**6.** Pepperoni _____   **7.** Cheese _____   **8.** Mushroom _____

---

**9.** Use the pictograph to estimate how much Angela's weekly income is from selling each kind of pizza. Each pizza cost $10.

cheese: _____   pepperoni: _____

mushroom: _____   other: _____

**10.** Based on how much Angela's weekly income is, estimate how much

Angela's monthly income is. _____

**11.** Estimate how much Angela's yearly income is. _____

# CONSTRUCTING A PICTOGRAPH

Karleen took a survey to find out how much money her friends spent each week at camp. Use her data to make a pictograph.

| Money Campers Spent Each Week |
| --- |
| • Esteban: $20    • Boris: $15 |
| • Shalandra: $35    • Marta: $40 |

To make a pictograph of this data, first choose a picture symbol to represent the amount of money spent. It should be simple and easy to draw. You could use $.

Next, decide the money value of the picture symbol. For this pictograph, each symbol is worth $10.

Now replace the money amounts with the symbols. For example, Shalandra spent $35. This is equal to

$$\frac{35}{10} = 3\frac{1}{2} \text{ symbols}$$

In pictograph form, Shalandra's spending is:

$$
\begin{array}{rl}
3 \text{ symbols} \longrightarrow & \$ \quad \$ \quad \$ \\
+ \ \frac{1}{2} \text{ symbols} \longrightarrow & \quad\quad\quad\quad\quad \text{\textcent} \\
\hline
3\frac{1}{2} \text{ symbols} &
\end{array}
$$

To construct a pictograph, list the campers' names vertically. Title the graph, and show the amount that the symbol represents along the bottom of the graph. The symbols for Shalandra are drawn next to her name.

### Money Campers Spent Each Week

| Esteban | |
| --- | --- |
| Shalandra | $ $ $ ¢ |
| Boris | |
| Marta | |

$ = $10

1. Use the data to figure out how many symbols to use on the pictograph to represent how much money Esteban, Boris, and Marta each spent.

   **a.** Divide the amount Esteban spent by 10. _____

   **b.** Add the information to the graph.

2. **a.** Divide the amount Boris spent by 10. _____

   **b.** Add the information to the graph.

3. **a.** Divide the amount Marta spent by 10. _____

   **b.** Add the information to the graph.

## Exercises

Over the entire summer, Karleen spent $260 at camp. Here is how she spent it.

4. Make a pictograph on a separate piece of paper to represent how much Karleen spent on different items.

| What Karleen Bought: |
| --- |
| • Food . . . . . . . . . . . . . . . .$145 |
| • Books . . . . . . . . . . . . . .$ 40 |
| • CDs . . . . . . . . . . . . . . .$ 55 |
| • Postcard/stamps . . . . . . .$ 20 |

## Application

5. What picture symbol did you choose to use in your pictograph? What amount does it represent? Explain why you chose this amount.

   _____

   _____

   _____

6. Think about how you spend money. What items do you buy? Collect the data and decide how you would represent it on a pictograph. Draw the pictograph on a separate sheet of paper.

# INTERPRETING A LINE GRAPH

## Vocabulary

**line graph:** a graph that shows changes in data over a period of time

**data point:** a point that shows a measurement

### *Reminder*

The vertical axis runs up and down the left side of a graph. The horizontal axis runs across the top or bottom of graph.

A **line graph** is used when you want to show changes in data over a period of time. The line graph below shows a month-by-month record of Pablo's weight. How much weight had Pablo lost by the end of the first month of his diet?

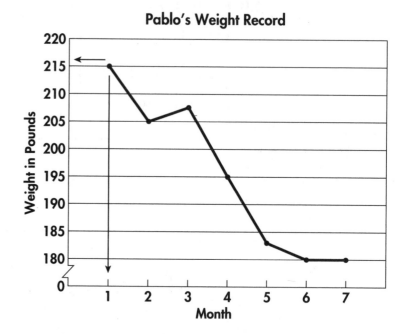

Look at the arrows on the graph. They show how to line up each **data point** with the vertical and horizontal scale.

For the first point, the horizontal scale lines up with 1 month. The vertical scale lines up with 215 pounds. This means that at the beginning of month 1, Pablo weighed 215 pounds.

To find out how much weight Pablo lost by the end of the first month of the diet, line up the vertical and horizontal scales for month 2.

*Weight change = month 2 weight – month 1 weight*
*= 215 pounds – 205 pounds*
*= 10 pounds*

Here's how you can use a line graph to spot trends in the weight record.

- A falling slope indicates a weight loss.
- A rising slope indicates a weight gain.
- A steep slope indicates a sharp loss or gain.
- A flat slope indicates no change in weight.

1. How much did Pablo weigh at the beginning of month 5? _____

   a. Find month 5 on the horizontal axis.

   b. Line up the data point with the vertical axis.

   c. Write Pablo's weight. _____

2. During which month did Pablo gain weight? _____

   a. Find a rising slope between two points.

   b. Write the name of the month. _____

   c. How much weight did Pablo gain? _____

## Exercises

**Use the graph on page 16 to answer these questions.**

3. What was Pablo's weight at the beginning of the:

   a. 6th month? _____   b. 7th month? _____   c. 4th month? _____

4. In which month did Pablo:

   a. lose about 12 pounds? _____

   b. lose about 3 pounds? _____

   c. lose nothing? _____

5. In which month did Pablo:

   a. lose the least? _____

   b. gain weight? _____

   c. stay the same? _____

## Application

6. What was the overall shape of the graph? Was it mainly a flat, rising, or falling slope? Explain what the shape means.

   _____

   _____

7. About how many pounds did Pablo lose in all? _____

# CONSTRUCTING A LINE GRAPH

Chuck collected these average monthly high temperature readings for Chicago.

### Chuck's Windy City Weather Data

| Dec. | Jan. | Feb. | Mar. | Apr. | May | Jun. | Jul. | Aug. | Sep. | Oct. | Nov. |
|------|------|------|------|------|-----|------|------|------|------|------|------|
| 28 | 21 | 26 | 36 | 49 | 59 | 69 | 73 | 72 | 65 | 54 | 40 |

To construct a line graph for this data, first make a vertical axis and a horizontal axis. Draw a scale on the vertical axis that represents the temperatures. A scale from 0° to 80° is about right. Then write the months of the year on the horizontal axis.

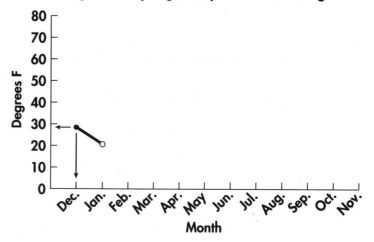

To graph data points:

1. Line up the first month on the horizontal scale. Notice how the arrow lines up with December.

2. Line up the temperature on the vertical scale. December's average temperature was 28 degrees.

3. Draw a point where the two imaginary lines meet.

4. Repeat the process for January.

5. Draw a line to connect the two points.

1. Graph February on the graph on page 18.

   **a.** What is February's average temperature? _____

   **b.** Line up this temperature with February on the horizontal axis. Draw a data point. Then draw a line to connect this point with the point for January.

## Exercises

2. Use the data in Chuck's table. Complete the graph on page 18 for Chicago.

## Application

3. Use the data in this table to make a temperature graph for Los Angeles.

### Average Monthly High Temperatures in Los Angeles

| Dec. | Jan. | Feb. | Mar. | Apr. | May | Jun. | Jul. | Aug. | Sep. | Oct. | Nov. |
|------|------|------|------|------|-----|------|------|------|------|------|------|
| 58   | 57   | 59   | 60   | 62   | 65  | 69   | 74   | 75   | 73   | 69   | 63   |

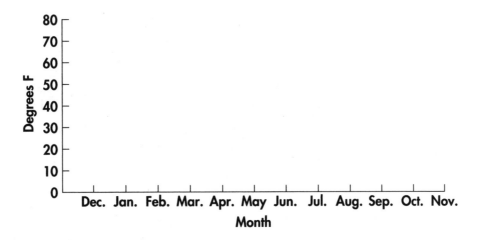

4. Compare the temperature patterns in Chicago and Los Angeles. Which city shows more change in its temperature pattern? Explain.

   _____

   _____

   _____

# DOUBLE LINE GRAPHS

## Vocabulary

**double line graph:** a line graph that compares two sets of data

The Yellow Dogs released a rock CD and a rap CD at the same time. To chart their sales, they used a **double line graph**. A double line graph compares two sets of data on the same line graph. Which CD is having better sales?

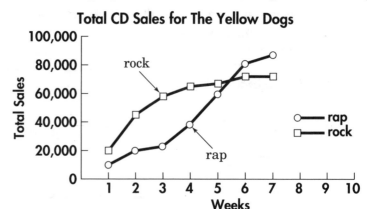

This graph shows total weekly sales for each CD.

The data points for the rap CD are shown as circles.

The data points for the rock CD are shown as squares.

You can see that the rap CD sales started slowly. They finally went ahead of the rock CD sales during week 5. You can tell this because the two lines cross. From that time on, the rap CD sold better than the rock CD.

The close-up below shows how to measure total sales at any point on the graph.

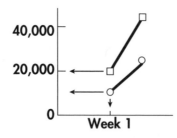

During week 1, the rock CD was ahead. It sold about 20,000 copies.

The rap CD sold about 10,000 copies.

## Guided Practice

1. Compare total sales for week 4.

   **a.** Which CD was ahead? _____

   **b.** What was the total for the rock CD? _____

   **c.** What was the total for the rap CD? _____

**2.** How many more rock CDs than rap CDs were sold in week 5?

_____

**Use the graph on page 20 to solve problems 3 to 9.**

**3.** Graph this data for week 8 on the graph on page 20: Rock: 81,000 Rap: 90,000

**4.** When did the rock CD have its biggest lead? _____

**5.** In which week was each CD selling at its best? _____

**6.** Which CD is selling faster? Point out a trend you can see. Explain how the graph supports the trend that you see.

_____

_____

_____

During which week was the rock CD sales total:

**7.** farthest ahead?      **8.** farthest behind?      **9.** equal to the rap total?

_____      _____      _____

**10.** Use data from the newspaper weather page to make a double line graph. Get the expected high and low temperatures for a 3-to 5-day forecast. Use one line for the high temperature and another for the low temperature. Graph the data on a double line graph.

**11.** Discuss weather trends you see on your graph in the space below. What were the highest two temperatures? The lowest? Point out at least two important trends that you see. Explain how your graph supports each trend.

_____

_____

_____

# INTERPRETING A CIRCLE GRAPH

## Vocabulary

**circle graph:** a graph in which data is presented as parts of a circle

### *Reminder*

You can change a percent to a fraction by dividing it by 100.

Blockbuster Video has three different divisions—video, film, and music. The **circle graph** shows how much money Blockbuster made from each division in a recent year. About what fractional part of Blockbuster's income came from music?

**Blockbuster Sales**

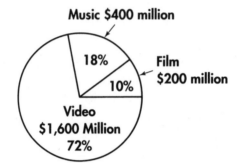

This circle represents Blockbuster's total income. It is divided into three parts. Each part represents a division of Blockbuster's business.

To determine what fractional part of Blockbuster's income came from music, you can look at the circle graph and see that 18%, or $400 million, of Blockbuster's income came from music. You can then make a rough estimate by comparing the size of the music section to the whole circle. You can see that music is less than one-fourth of the whole circle. To get a more accurate fractional estimate, you can:

1. Round off 18% to 20%.

2. Change 20% to a fraction: $20\% = \frac{20}{100}$

3. Express in simplest terms: $\frac{20}{100} = \frac{2}{10} = \frac{1}{5}$

You can conclude that about $\frac{1}{5}$ of Blockbuster's total sales came from music.

To find Blockbuster's total income, you can add the amounts in each part of the graph.

$200 million + $400 million + $1,600 million = $2,200 million

## Guided Practice

1. What percent of Blockbuster's income was earned by its largest division? _____

   **a.** Write the name of the division. _____

   **b.** Write the dollar amount. _____

   **c.** Write the percent amount. _____

2. Change the percent amount in 1c to a fraction. _____

   **a.** Round off the percent total. _____

   **b.** Express the percent as a fraction. _____

   **c.** Express the fraction in simplest terms. _____

## Exercises

 **Use the circle graph and a calculator to solve problems 3 to 6.**

**Monthly Viewing Expenses**

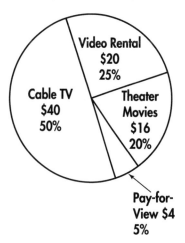

3. Which viewing expense was one-fifth of the total? _____

4. What was the total amount spent per month? _____

5. What percent of the total was spent inside the home? Outside the home?

   _____ _____

6. What fraction of the total amount was spent on cable TV and video rental? _____

## Application

7. Think about what you and your family spend for cable TV, video rentals, and movies. Estimate the fraction of the total amount of your viewing expenses that you spend on each.

_____

# MEASURING CENTRAL ANGLES IN A CIRCLE GRAPH

## Vocabulary

**angle:** two rays with a common endpoint

**central angle:** an angle whose vertex is the center of a circle

**sector:** a part of a circle graph formed by a central angle

### *Reminder*

A complete circle has 360 degrees.

Nita was the movie reviewer for her school paper. She made a circle graph to show the results of 24 movies she reviewed. How could you find the fraction that the "No Opinion" sector shows?

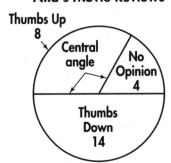

**Nita's Movie Reviews**

**Angles** mark off the boundaries of each sector in the circle graph. The size of each **sector** is determined by the fraction that it shows.

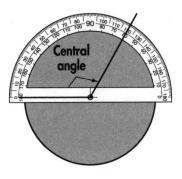

You can measure the **central angle** of the "Thumbs Up" sector with a protractor.

1. Place the protractor over the angle as shown.

2. Line up the center of the circle with the center lines of the protractor.

3. Read the measure of the angle. It measures 120 degrees.

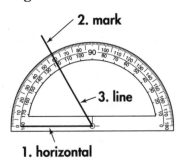

To draw an angle of 60 degrees:

1. Draw a horizontal ray.

2. Place the protractor over the line as shown. Make a mark at 60 degrees.

3. Draw a ray to complete the sector.

To find what fractional part the "No Opinion" sector shows, you can do the following to find the simplest form of a fraction:

$$\frac{60}{360} = \frac{60}{360} = \frac{1}{6}$$

with $\div 60$ shown on top and $\div 60$ shown on bottom.

The fractional part of the "No Opinion" sector is $\frac{1}{6}$.

## Guided Practice

1. Measure the central angle for "No Opinion."

   **a.** Place the protractor over the angle.

   **b.** Line up the protractor's center lines with the center of the circle.

   **c.** Read the measure of the angle. Write its measure. _____

2. The angle for "Thumbs Up" takes up 120 degrees of the circle.

   **a.** Find the fraction that this sector shows.

   **b.** Write the fraction of the entire circle. _____

## Exercises

Bob saw 36 movies. This circle graph shows what kinds of movies Bob saw.

**Use a protractor to measure angles represented by:**

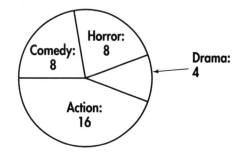

3. comedies _____ 4. action movies _____ 5. dramas _____

6. What is the fractional part for the drama sector? _____

## Application

7. Imagine you saw 12 movies last month: 6 comedies, 3 action, and 3 horror. An angle of 180 degrees represents the number of comedies you saw. How many degrees represent each of the other kinds of movies?

_____

8. What is the fractional part for each of the sectors for problem 7? _____

# CONSTRUCTING A CIRCLE GRAPH

## Reminder

The size of an angle in a circle graph is based on the relationship between the amount the angle represents and the whole amount pictured by the graph.

New Jersey's population of about 8 million people can be broken down into 3 age groups. How could you find the percentage for the population under 17?

| Age Group | Under 17 | 18–64 | 65 + |
|---|---|---|---|
| Population | 1.9 million | 4.9 million | 1.1 million |
| Percent | | | |
| Angle | | | |

To make a circle graph from this data, first find the percent of the total that each age group represents. The total population for New Jersey is 7.9 million. For the under-17 group:

$$1.9 \div 7.9 \approx 0.24$$

$$0.24 \times 100 = 24\%$$

The percentage of the population for under 17 is 24%. Twenty-four percent of the circle should be taken up by the under-17 group. The entire circle has 360 degrees. So the size of the central angle for the under-17 group is:

$$0.24 \times 360 = 86 \text{ or } 86°$$

**New Jersey Population by Age**

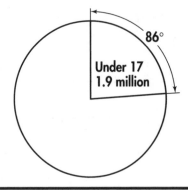

To draw a central angle of 86 degrees, first draw a circle. Draw a horizontal ray.

Use a protractor to measure 86 degrees. Make a mark.

Draw the angle. Label this part of the circle graph.

## Guided Practice

1. Construct the 18-to-64 age group in the circle graph above.

   **a.** Write the population in the 18-to-64 age group.

   _____

**b.** Find the percent of the total that this age group represents.

_____

**c.** Find the central angle measure that shows this percent.

_____

**d.** Use a protractor to draw the central angle and then label this part of the circle graph.

## Exercises

**2.** Complete the data from New York State in the following table.

| Age Group | Under 17 | 18–64 | 65 + |
|---|---|---|---|
| Population | 4.5 | 11.3 | 2.4 |
| Percentage | | | |
| Angle | | | |

**New York State Population by Age Group**

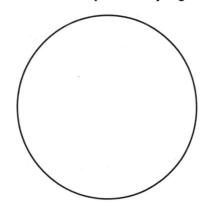

**3.** Use the data from problem 2 to complete the circle graph above.

## Application

**4.** Colorado has a population of 3.3 million. Based on the New York and New Jersey data, how many people from Colorado would you expect to be 17 or younger? Explain how you got your answer.

_____

_____

## INTERPRETING A HISTOGRAM

### Vocabulary

**histogram:** a bar graph that shows groups of data

In the gymnastics competition, four gymnasts competed in four different events. The gymnasts' scores are listed below. What is a typical score for the gymnasts?

|  | Events | | | |
|---|---|---|---|---|
|  | Vault | Bar | Beam | Floor Work |
| **1** | 5.125 | 5.150 | 5.125 | 5.075 |
| **2** | 7.650 | 5.450 | 5.975 | 6.975 |
| **3** | 6.450 | 6.875 | 8.350 | 8.650 |
| **4** | 9.125 | 9.375 | 8.250 | 8.750 |

A **histogram** shows groups of data. The histogram below graphs the data from the above table.

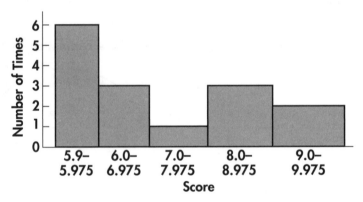

The vertical axis shows the number of times the gymnasts received a a score. The horizontal axis shows the scores. To find out how many times the gymnasts received a score between 5.0–5.975, line up the the 5.0–5.975 bar with the scale. You can see that these were the most typical scores.

---

### Guided Practice

1. What were the gymnasts' least common scores?

   **a.** Find the shortest bar.

   **b.** How many times did the gymnasts receive a score in this range? _____

Students at the Post Road School measured the size of their arm span from fingertip to fingertip. The table shows the results.

| Inches | Number of Students | Inches | Number of Students | Inches | Number of Students | Inches | Number of Students | Inches | Number of Students |
|---|---|---|---|---|---|---|---|---|---|
| 56 | 1 | 61 |  | 66 | 1 | 71 | 3 | 76 |  |
| 57 | 1 | 62 | 1 | 67 | 3 | 72 | 1 | 77 | 1 |
| 58 |  | 63 | 1 | 68 | 4 | 73 |  | 78 | 1 |
| 58 | 1 | 64 | 2 | 69 | 1 | 74 | 3 | 79 |  |
| 60 | 2 | 65 | 3 | 70 | 2 | 75 | 1 | 80 |  |

**2.** Use the information on the table to graph the arm span of students.

Number of Sudents

56–60        61–65        66–70        71–75        76–80

Inches

What size arm span was:

**3.** most common?            **4.** least common?            **5.** second most common?

_____            _____            _____

**6.** What percent of the students have arm spans between 64 and 71 inches? What percent have arm spans below 60 inches? above 75 inches?

_____

_____

COOPERATIVE

LEARNING

**7.** Work with a partner to analyze the histogram. What patterns do you see?

_____

_____

# FINDING THE MEAN AND RANGE

## Vocabulary

**range:** a measure of how spread out the data values are; computed by finding the difference between the greatest value and the least value

**mean:** the average that is calculated by dividing the sum of the values by the number of values

Officer O'Rourke wrote out these parking and traffic tickets over a period of 8 days. What is the average number of parking tickets that he wrote per day?

| Day | 1 | 2 | 3 | 4 | 5 | 6 | 7 | 8 |
|---|---|---|---|---|---|---|---|---|
| Parking Tickets | 12 | 19 | 16 | 13 | 15 | 9 | 10 | 20 |
| Traffic Tickets | 5 | 11 | 0 | 10 | 9 | 4 | 6 | 5 |

The **range** gives you a rough idea of how the number varied from day to day. The number of parking tickets varied from 9 (low) to 20 (high).

$$range = 20 - 9 = 11$$

The number of tickets varied by 11.

The **mean** gives you an idea of how many parking tickets Officer O'Rourke wrote on an average day during this time period. To calculate the mean, first add up the number of parking tickets on your calculator.

Total: 12 ⊞ 19 ⊞ 16 ⊞ 13 ⊞ 15 ⊞ 9 ⊞ 10 ⊞ 20 = 114

You have eight values, one for each day. Divide by eight.

114 ÷ 8 = 14.25 parking tickets

## Guided Practice

1. Find the range for the number of traffic tickets O'Rourke wrote. Then use your calculator to find the mean number of traffic tickets.

   **a.** Range: find the difference between the highest and lowest amounts. _____

   **b.** Mean: first find the total number of tickets.

   _____

   **c.** Divide by the number of values (days).

   _____

## Exercises

The table shows how much the people who work at Roy's Diner paid in parking fines last year.

| | Ming | Johnny | DeWayne | Fatima | Roy | Rita |
|---|---|---|---|---|---|---|
| **Tickets** | 7 | 3 | 5 | 0 | 12 | 9 |
| **Fines** | $125 | $40 | $80 | $0 | $425 | $145 |

**For the number of tickets, find the:**

**2.** range. ____________

**3.** total number of tickets for everyone. ____________

**4.** mean. ____________

**For parking fines, find the:**

**5.** range. ____________

**6.** total fines paid by everyone. ____________

**7.** mean (to the nearest dollar). ____________

**8.** Roy is the owner of the diner. The other five people are employees. Find the mean for the employees. ____________

## Application

**9.** Explain why the mean changed so much when Roy's fines weren't included.

______________________________________________

______________________________________________

______________________________________________

**10.** Look at the range and the mean for parking tickets and fines for the six people at the diner. Did the mean for parking tickets fall closer to the high end or the low end of the range?

______________________________________________

______________________________________________

______________________________________________

# FINDING THE MEDIAN AND THE MODE

## Vocabulary

**median:** central value for a set of data

**mode:** most common value for a set of data

## Reminder

The mean is the average value of a set of data.

The table shows Oliver's rebounds and point totals over 11 basketball games. How can you get an idea of how well Oliver rebounded in a typical game?

| Game | 1 | 2 | 3 | 4 | 5 | 6 | 7 | 8 | 9 | 10 | 11 |
|---|---|---|---|---|---|---|---|---|---|---|---|
| Rebounds | 13 | 12 | 9 | 14 | 2 | 9 | 16 | 10 | 14 | 19 | 9 |
| Point Totals | 14 | 19 | 9 | 20 | 6 | 15 | 19 | 19 | 17 | 26 | 16 |

In order to find out how well Oliver rebounded in a typical game, you can find the median and mode for his rebounding totals.

The **median** is the center value for a set of data. To find the median, arrange the data by size. The central value is the median.

2   9   9   9   10   12   13   14   14   16   19
  these 5            median            these 5
 are smaller                          are larger

Half the values were larger than the median. The other half were smaller than the median. The median is 12.

The **mode** is the most common value in the data. In this case, the value of 9 occurs three times. The mode is 9.

## Guided Practice

1. Find the mode for Oliver's point totals.

   **a.** Find the value that occurs most often.

   _____

   **b.** Write the mode here. _____

2. Find the median for Oliver's point totals.

   **a.** Arrange the scores by size. _____

   **b.** Find the central value. _____

   **c.** Write the median here. _____

9 1 1 8 (1) 16 12 18 16   7.01

9 3 4 6 (6) 6 7 9 18   5.61

18 11 11 (12) 14 17 17 26 21  } 14.11

| NAME | | | | | | | |
|---|---|---|---|---|---|---|---|
| Alex Grezesiak (chec) | | | | | | | |
| Robert Haynes | | | | | | | |
| Ben Lakner | | | | | | | |
| Chet Pinder | | | | | | | |
| Matt VanHassel | | | | | | | |
| Paul Kutinsky | | | | | | | |
| Matt Edwards | | | | | | | |
| Stephanie Olsen | | | | | | | |
| Anthony Maiorana | | | | | | | |
| Paul Weston | | | | | | | |
| RJ Simmons | | | | | | | |
| | | | | | | | |
| Chris Bartlett | | | | | | | |
| Joe Falsarella | | | | | | | |
| Kevin Gallagher | | | | | | | |
| Morgan LaRock (Lib) | | | | | | | |
| Norbert Leppig (aide) | | | | | | | |
| Erica Dr... | | | | | | | |

Every day ←

Alex
?
"
?
?

The table gives scoring totals over 9 games for three different players.

|       | 1  | 2  | 3  | 4  | 5  | 6  | 7  | 8  | 9  |
|-------|----|----|----|----|----|----|----|----|----|
| Maya  | 7  | 12 | 9  | 5  | 7  | 16 | 10 | 15 | 8  |
| Tati  | 6  | 7  | 9  | 0  | 4  | 10 | 6  | 3  | 6  |
| Lydia | 11 | 14 | 11 | 12 | 20 | 17 | 11 | 10 | 21 |

**Find the mode for:**

3. Maya                    4. Tati                    5. Lydia

_____        _____        _____

**Find the median for:**

6. Maya                    7. Tati                    8. Lydia

_____        _____        _____

**Find the mean for:**

9. Maya                    10. Tati                   11. Lydia

_____        _____        _____

12. Compare the mean to the mode and the median for each player. Is the mean closer to the mode or the median?

_____

_____

_____

13. The starting salaries for baseball players on one team are $160,000, $160,000, $220,000, $330,000, $510,000, $890,000, $1,500,000, $2,800,000 and $3,800,000. The owners claim that a typical player (mean) on the team makes over 1 million dollars. The players claim that a typical player (median) makes about $500,000 annually. Which is a better representation and why?

_____

_____

_____

# CONSTRUCTING A STEM-AND-LEAF PLOT

## Vocabulary

**stem-and-leaf plot:** a method of grouping data by using place value

During the past 14 weeks, Jolette put in these hours at the Burger Factory restaurant. What was a typical week like for her?

*14, 18, 35, 41, 28, 21, 50, 26, 38, 21, 45, 23, 27, 30*

To find out, you could graph the data on a **stem-and-leaf plot.** A stem-and-leaf graph is like a histogram, but it is a quicker way to organize data into groups.

To construct a stem-and-leaf plot, first find the least and greatest value. The least value is 14. It has a 1 in the tens place. The greatest value is 50. It has a 5 in the tens place.

The stems will be the digits 1 through 5.

| stem | leaf |
|------|------|
| 1 | 4  8 |
| 2 | 8  1  6  1  3  7 |
| 3 | 5  8  0 |
| 4 | 1  5 |
| 5 | 0 |

Key: 1|4 means 14 hours

Now draw a vertical line to separate the tens and the ones. Then look at 14. The one is shown on the stem. Write the four to the right of the 1. To show 18, write the 8 to the right of the 1.

By looking at the stem-and leaf plot, you can quickly see that Jolette would usually spend between 20 and 30 hours per week at her job.

## Guided Practice

1. Show the number 47 on the stem-and-leaf plot.

   **a.** What is the stem for 47? _____

   **b.** What is the leaf for 47? _____

   **c.** Write the stem and leaf on the stem-and-leaf plot.

**Race Times (in seconds)**

```
5 | 9
6 | 7  1  4  6  9
7 | 2  3  2
8 | 4
```

Ten members of the track team ran the quarter mile on Tuesday. Their times are given in the stem-and-leaf plot.

## How many runners had times:

**2.** below 60 seconds?   **3.** between 70 and 80 seconds?   **4.** of exactly 72 seconds?

_____        _____              _____

## How many runners ran the race:

**5.** in all?          **6.** in less than 70 seconds?      **7.** in 70 seconds or more?

_____        _____              _____

**8.** On Wednesday, two new runners ran times of 76 and 65 seconds. Show this new data on the stem-and-leaf plot above.

24 people signed up for a bowling league. In the practice session, each person bowled one game. Here were the scores:

88, 165, 172, 136, 103, 163, 95, 178, 108, 112, 154, 172, 157, 83, 98, 171, 91, 109, 115, 131, 111, 181, 160, 99

**9.** Using the above data, construct a stem- and-leaf plot. Let 2|50 represent a score of 250. Then answer the following questions.

**a.** What is a typical score? _____

**b.** By looking at the stem-and-leaf plot, what would be some fair ways to create teams?

_____

_____

# CONSTRUCTING A SCATTERGRAM

## Vocabulary

**scattergram:** a graph that shows the relationship between two sets of data using points. Each point represents a pair of numbers.

**correlation:** the relationship between two sets of data

**line of best fit:** a straight line that is drawn through the scattergram that estimates the relationship between the two sets of data.

Concert tickets at the Palace Theater ranged from $5 to $100.

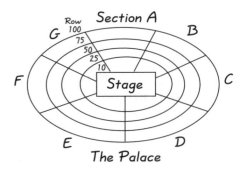

About buying concert tickets at the Palace, Rick thinks: "The farther you are from the stage, the less your tickets cost." Chantal isn't so sure. To find out, she collected six ticket stubs from Section A at a recent concert. How does the cost of seats change as the seats get farther from the stage? One set of data showed row tickets. The other set showed ticket prices.

| Section A | | | | | | |
|---|---|---|---|---|---|---|
| Ticket | 1 | 2 | 3 | 4 | 5 | 6 |
| Row | 20 | 60 | 12 | 80 | 48 | 40 |
| Ticket Price | $65 | $35 | $71 | $20 | $44 | $50 |

How was the ticket price related to row number?

To find out, Chantal graphed her data on a **scattergram**. A scattergram shows the relationship between two sets of data. Each point in a scattergram is represented by a pair of numbers. The horizontal axis represents one set of data while the vertical axis represents another set of data.

To graph ticket 1 from the table on the scattergram:

1. Line up with Row 20 on the horizontal axis.

2. Line up with $65 on the vertical axis. Draw a point where they meet.

3. Graph other points in a similar way.

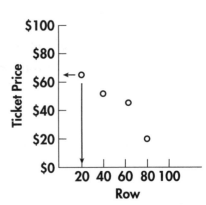

By looking at the scattergram, you can find out the type of **correlation.**
There are three types of correlation: [a] when one set of data increases, so
does the other (positive); [b] when one set of data increases, the other set
decreases (negative); or no relationships exist at all.

To find out what type of correlation there is on this scattergram, try to
draw a straight line (**line of best fit**) through the points so that the line is
as close to all the points as possible.

Notice how the line slants downward as
you move along it to the right. As the row
number gets larger, you can see that the
ticket price gets smaller. There is a negative
correlation between row number and ticket
price. This means that the tickets that are
farther away from the stage cost less.

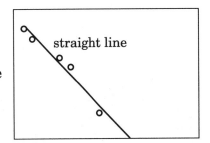

## Guided Practice

Chantal still had her doubts. She collected more data from Section C which
is shown on the table below.

| Section C | | | | | | |
|---|---|---|---|---|---|---|
| Ticket | 1 | 2 | 3 | 4 | 5 | 6 |
| Row | 20 | 60 | 2 | 80 | 48 | 12 |
| Ticket Price | $55 | $25 | $70 | $10 | $34 | $61 |

**1.** Identify the point that would appear on the far left side of the graph.

   **a.** Line up the point with the horizontal axis. Write the row number.

   _____

   **b.** Line up the point with the vertical axis. Write the ticket price.

   _____

   **c.** Which ticket does this show? _____

**2.** Graph ticket 4. Use the graph on page 36.

   **a.** Line up even with Row 80 on the horizontal axis.

   **b.** Line up even with a ticket price of $10 on the vertical axis.

   **c.** Draw a point on the graph where the two lines meet.

Chantal collected this data from Section E. Two of the points are graphed below.

| Section E | | | | | | |
|---|---|---|---|---|---|---|
| Ticket | 1 | 2 | 3 | 4 | 5 | 6 |
| Row | 20 | 60 | 2 | 80 | 48 | 12 |
| Ticket Price | $50 | $20 | $65 | $5 | $29 | $56 |

In the graph, the point on the left:

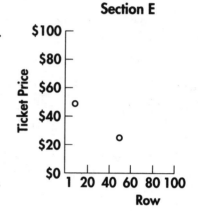

**3.** shows a ticket price of _____.

**4.** represents row _____.

**5.** shows ticket number _____.

The point on the right:

**6.** shows a ticket price of _____.

**7.** represents row _____.

**8.** shows ticket number _____.

Ticket number 4 would line up with:

**9.** Row 80 on the _____ axis.

**10.** A price of $5 on the _____ axis.

**11.** Graph the remaining tickets from section E on the graph above.

**12.** Chantal collected this data from different sections. Graph these points from different sections on the graph that follows.

| Ticket | 1 | 2 | 3 | 4 | 5 | 6 |
|---|---|---|---|---|---|---|
| Section | B | C | D | E | F | A |
| Row | 20 | 60 | 100 | 64 | 32 | 1 |
| Ticket Price | $60 | $25 | $5 | $17 | $46 | $100 |

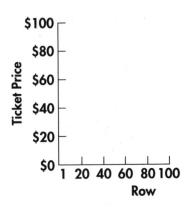

## Application

Collect data about the following: the shoe sizes and heights of 10 people. Then make a scattergram to show the two sets of data. Each point represents a person.

**13.** Before you graph the data, predict whether the set of data will show a positive, negative, or no correlation.

_____

_____

**14.** What conclusions can you draw from the data? Explain any correlation that you find.

_____

_____

# MISLEADING GRAPHS

Have you ever seen ads like this one?

**Which would you rather pay for your next phone call?**

**Kidd  Diamond**
Cost of a 3-minute long distance call

**There IS a difference in phone companies.**

A **BIG** difference.

Kidd Long Distance

**No Kidding**

This ad may sound pretty convincing. Take a close look at the graph. Notice that it doesn't have a scale.

In fact, the graph above is really just a closeup view of the very top portion of the graph shown below on the left. Once you put in a complete scale the savings don't look so big anymore.

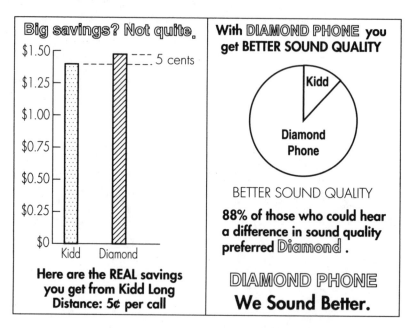

**Big savings? Not quite.**

$1.50 ----- 5 cents
$1.25
$1.00
$0.75
$0.50
$0.25
$0
  Kidd   Diamond

**Here are the REAL savings you get from Kidd Long Distance: 5¢ per call**

**With DIAMOND PHONE you get BETTER SOUND QUALITY**

Kidd

Diamond Phone

BETTER SOUND QUALITY

**88% of those who could hear a difference in sound quality preferred Diamond.**

DIAMOND PHONE
**We Sound Better.**

In fact, the circle graph in the Diamond ad is misleading too. What Diamond didn't say was that most people couldn't hear a difference in phone reception. This circle graph below gives the data.

Ninety-eight percent of all customers couldn't hear a difference in sound quality between Kidd and Diamond.

This means that Diamond's circle graph gave data for just a tiny group of people—the 2% who could hear a difference in sound quality between phone companies.

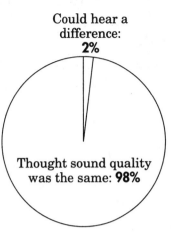

Could hear a difference: **2%**

Thought sound quality was the same: **98%**

## Guided Practice

**1.** In the first ad:

    **a.** Which bar appears to be larger? _____

    **b.** How many times as large as the other bar does it appear to be?

    _____

    **c.** Suppose a phone call using Kidd cost 50 cents. Use Kidd's graph to estimate how much you would expect the same call to cost on

    Diamond. _____

**2.** In the bar graph part of the Diamond ad:

    **a.** Which bar was larger? _____

    **b.** How much larger was it than the other bar?

    _____

    **c.** Suppose a phone call using Kidd cost 50 cents. Use Diamond's graph to estimate how much you would expect the same call to cost on

    Diamond. _____

**3.** In the circle graph part of the Diamond ad:

    **a.** What percent could hear a difference in reception? _____

    **b.** Of those people, what percent thought Diamond's reception was

    better? _____

    **c.** Estimate how many people out of 100 would prefer Diamond's

    reception. _____

Misleading graphs give you only part of the picture. Compare the graphs below for how many complaints each company gets.

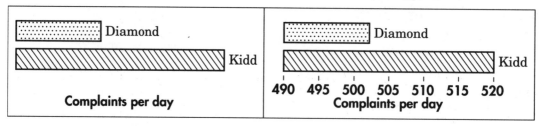

| Part of the picture | The whole picture |
|---|---|

From the graph above, it appears that Kidd:

**4.** had more/fewer complaints. _____

**5.** was more/less reliable. _____

**6.** had about _____ as many complaints.

**Use the graph above to estimate the answers.**

**7.** Kidd had about _____ more complaints than Diamond.

**8.** Kidd had a total of about _____ complaints.

**9.** Kidd had about _____% more complaints than Diamond.

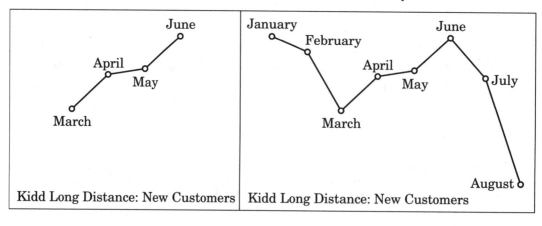

| Part of the picture | The whole picture |
|---|---|

**The graph above shows:**

**10.** the months from _____ to _____.

**11.** new customers to be increasing/decreasing. _____

**12.** the most new customers in the month of _____.

**The graph on page 42 shows:**

**13.** new customers to be _____.

**14.** the most new customers in _____.

**15.** the fewest new customers in _____.

## Application

**16.** Draw a new complaint graph using the data from the bar graphs above. This time, start the scale at 0 rather than at 490. How does this graph change the way the data looks? What was misleading about the original bar graphs?

_____

_____

_____

**17.** What was misleading about the new customer graphs? Why do you think the company presented them this way?

_____

_____

_____

**18.** How can you look out for misleading graphs in the future?

_____

_____

_____

# APPLICATIONS: USING TABLES

NBA Basketball standings for the Midwest Division on March 24 are shown below. This table gives you many different kinds of information including:

| Team | Won | Lost | Percent-age | Games Behind | Last 10 Games | Streak |
|------|-----|------|-------------|--------------|---------------|--------|
| Utah | 50 | 18 | .735 | — | 8-2 | Won 2 |
| San Antonio | 46 | 18 | .719 | 2 | 8-2 | Won 5 |
| Houston | 40 | 26 | .606 | 9 | 5-5 | Lost 2 |
| Denver | 31 | 35 | .470 | 18 | 6-4 | Lost 2 |
| Dallas | 28 | 37 | .431 | 20.5 | 6-4 | Won 3 |
| Minnesota | 19 | 48 | .284 | 30.5 | 3-7 | Lost 1 |

- Each team's win and loss record.
- The percentage of games won. This is written as a decimal.
- The number of games each team is behind the leader. Suppose a team is 2 games behind the leader. It can move into a tie for first place if it wins 2 games and the leader loses 2 games.
- A record of how the team did over the last 10 games. A record of 8-2 stands for 8 wins, 2 losses.
- A streak record showing how many games in a row the team has recently won or lost.

## Guided Practice

1. Which team has the best overall record?

   a. Write the name of the team in first place.

   _____

   b. How many more games has it won than the second place team? _____

   c. How many fewer games has it lost than the second place team? _____

2. Which team has the best streak? _____

**Use the Midwest Division standings to answer these questions.**

Which team or teams have:

**3.** lost the most games in a row? _____

**4.** won more than they've lost? _____

**5.** lost more games than they've won? _____

**6.** played the most games? _____

**7.** won about half their games? _____

**8.** won 14 more games than they lost? _____

**9.** How many games behind is Houston? _____

**10.** Which team is closest to catching up with the team ahead of it? Which team is farthest behind the team ahead of it? Explain your answers.

_____

_____

**Application**

**11.** Suppose Utah loses its next 3 games and San Antonio wins its next 3 games. Which team will have more wins? More losses? Which will be in first place? Explain your answer.

_____

_____

**12.** Which team do you think will finish first in the Midwest Division? Explain your answer.

_____

_____

# USING GRAPHS

Everyone agrees: Hector's Super Salsa tastes terrific. Can Hector make money selling his salsa at $2.50 a jar? Here is a record of his sales.

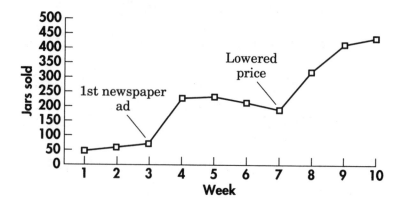

You can see from the graph that sales were slow until Hector took out weekly newspaper ads. The ads cost $200 per week. How did the ads affect sales?

Line up the points for week 3 and week 4. You can see that sales jumped from about 60 jars to about 230 jars.

Was the newspaper ad a good decision? Here you need to compare net income from week 3 and week 4.

Week 3 = Number of jars × cost of jar
       = 60 jars × $2.50
       = $150

Week 4 = (Number of jars × cost of jar)
         – cost of ad
       = (230 jars × $2.50) – $200
       = $575 – $200
       = $375

When you compare net incomes from week 3 and week 4, you see that taking out the ad looks like a good idea so far.

$375 (Week 4) – $150 (Week 3) = $325
                more net income

## Guided Practice

1. Find the net income for week 5 including a $200 ad.

   a. Write the number of jars that sold for week 5.

   _____

**b.** Multiply number of jars by $2.50. _____

**c.** Subtract $200 for the cost of the ad. _____

2. Compare the net income for week 6 to week 5.

    **a.** Multiply number of jars for week 6 by $2.50. _____

    **b.** Subtract the cost of the ad for week 6. _____

    **c.** Compare net income for week 6 to week 5.

_____

## Exercises

At the beginning of week 7, Hector lowered the price of Super Salsa from $2.50 per jar to $1.50 per jar.

### At $1.50 a jar for week 8 Hector:

**3.** sold how many jars? _____

**4.** paid how much for ads? _____

**5.** had how much net income? _____

### During week 9, Hector:

**6.** sold how many jars? _____

**7.** paid how much for ads? _____

**8.** had how much net income? _____

## Application

9. During what two weeks did Super Salsa bring in the most income? How much income did it bring in during each of these weeks?

_____

10. Were the newspaper ads worth their cost? Explain.

_____

_____

# GRAPHING ORDERED PAIRS

## Vocabulary

**coordinate system:** a grid that is used to map points on the x-axis and y-axis

**x-axis:** the horizontal axis

**y-axis:** the vertical axis

**ordered pair:** two numbers that map a point on a coordinate system

A grid like the one shown below is called a **coordinate system**. A coordinate system maps a point by showing its relationship to the **x-axis** (horizontal axis) and **y-axis** (vertical axis). Each axis starts at zero. How can you use an ordered pair to locate a point on the grid?

Along the x-axis, positive numbers go to the right. Negative numbers go the left.

Along the y-axis, positive numbers go up. Negative numbers go down.

Each point on the grid can be located with an **ordered pair.**

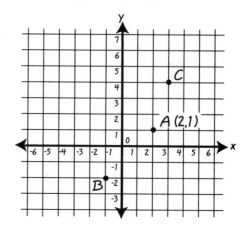

An ordered pair has two values—an x-value and a y-value. The x-value always comes first.

Example: The ordered pair (2,1) gives the location of point A. It has an x-value of $^+2$ and a y-value of $^+1$. From the center point (0,0), point A is:

> 2 units to the right on the x-axis
> 1 unit up on the y-axis

Another example: Draw a point that is located at ($^-1,^-2$).

Start at center point (0,0).
Move 1 unit left. Move 2 units down. The ordered pair ($^-1,^-2$) is located at point B.

## Guided Practice

1. What ordered pair gives the location of point C?

   **a.** Line up point C with the x-axis. Write the x-value. _____

   **b.** Line up point C with the y-axis. Write the y-value. _____

   **c.** Write the ordered pair. _____

**2.** Draw point Q that is located at (⁻3,2).

    **a.** Start at center point (0,0).

    **b.** Move 3 units left on the x-axis.

    **c.** Move 2 units up and draw point Q.

## Exercises

**Write an ordered pair for each point on the coordinate system above.**

**3.** Point D _____

**4.** Point E _____

**5.** Point F _____

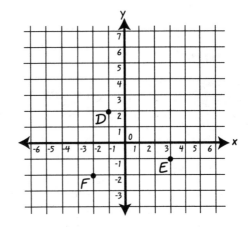

**Use these ordered pairs to draw points G, H, and I:**

**6.** Point G: (4,2)        **7.** Point H: (⁻4,3)        **8.** Point I: (5,⁻2)

_____        _____        _____

## Application

**9.** Draw these ordered pairs on a coordinate system: (1,3), (3,1), (3,⁻2), (⁻1,⁻2), (⁻1,1). Connect the first point to the second, the second to the third, and so on. What familiar shape did you draw?

_____

COOPERATIVE

LEARNING

**10.** Choose any lower-case letter in the alphabet. Use ordered pairs to draw the letter on a coordinate system. Then write directions for how to connect the ordered pairs. Trade with a classmate. See if you can find out the letters.

_____

_____

**11.** Draw a line segment whose endpoints are: (2,3), (3,2). Now draw a second segment that is parallel to the first. Use ordered pairs to name its endpoints.

_____

# GRAPHING A LINEAR EQUATION

## Vocabulary

**linear equation:** an equation that can be graphed as a straight line on a coordinate system

## *Reminder*

The x-value always comes first in an ordered pair. Ordered pairs are two numbers that map a point on a coordinate system

A **linear equation** can be graphed as a line on a coordinate system. A linear equation has two unknowns, usually $x$ and $y$. Any $x$ and $y$ pair that makes the equation true also tells you a point that is on the graph of the equation.

What does the graph of $y = 2x + 1$ look like? You can use the equation $y = 2x + 1$ as a rule that tells every ordered pair that is on its graph. To graph the linear equation, you need to locate points that are on the graph. Here's how to do it.

| | |
|---|---|
| Write the equation. | $y = 2x + 1$ |
| Take any value of $x$ you want, such as $x = 1$. Substitute 1 for $x$ into the equation. | $y = 2(1) + 1$ |
| Find the value that $y$ takes. | $y = 3$ |
| This can be written as an ordered pair to show $x = 1$ and $y = 3$. | $(1, 3)$ |

$(1, 3)$ can be drawn as an ordered pair on the graph.

| x | y |
|---|---|
| 1 | 3 |

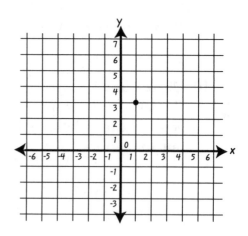

Repeat the process one or more times. Use a different value for x.

$$y = 2(2) + 1$$
$$y = 5$$

Write the ordered pair that results.

(2, 5)

Graph the ordered pairs on a coordinate system.

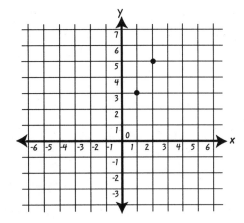

Draw a line through the two points. Any point on the line is a solution of $y = 2x + 1$.

| x | y |
|---|---|
| 1 | 3 |
| 2 | 5 |

## Guided Practice

1. Find the value of $y$ when $x = 3$.

   **a.** Put $x = 3$ into the equation $y = 2(3) + 1$.

   **b.** Write the value for $x$ and $y$ in the table. _____

   **c.** Write and graph the ordered pair on the above coordinate system.

2. Find the value of $y$ when $x = 0$.

   **a.** Put $x = 0$ into the equation $y = 2(0) + 1$.

   **b.** Write the value for $x$ and $y$ in the table. _____

   **c.** Write and graph the ordered pair on the above coordinate system.

   **d.** Draw a line through the three points.

3. Find the value of $y$ when $x = -1$.

   **a.** Put $x = -1$ into the equation $y = 2(-2) + 1$.

   **b.** Write the value for $x$ and $y$ in the table. _____ (–1, –3)

   **c.** Write and graph the ordered pair on the above coordinate system.

   **d.** Draw a line through the four points.

4. Are all the points on the same line? _____

For the equation, $y = x - 5$, write a $y$-value for each value of $x$.

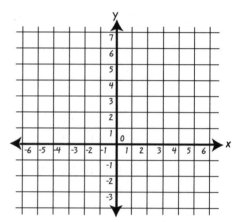

**5. a.** When $x = 8$, $y =$ _____

   **b.** When $x = 6$, $y =$ _____

   **c.** When $x = 3$, $y =$ _____

   **d.** Write the three ordered pairs you found. _____

   **e.** Graph the three ordered pairs on the above coordinate system.

   **f.** Draw a straight line through the points you made.

For the equation, $y = 3x - 2$, write a $y$-value for each value of $x$.

**6. a.** When $x = 2$, $y =$ _____ .

   **b.** When $x = 3$, $y =$ _____ .

   **c.** When $x = -1$, $y =$ _____ .

   **d.** Write the three ordered pairs you found. _____

   **e.** Graph the three ordered pairs on the above coordinate system.

   **f.** Draw a straight line through the points you made.

**7.** For the equation, $y = 4x - 3$, write a $y$-value for each value of $x$.

   **a.** When $x = 0$, $y =$ _____ .

   **b.** When $x = -1$, $y =$ _____ .

   **c.** When $x = 1$, $y =$ _____ .

   **d.** Write the three ordered pairs you found. _____

   **e.** Graph the three ordered pairs on the above coordinate system.

   **f.** Draw a straight line through the points you made.

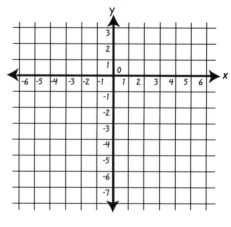

**8.** Try graphing these three equations on the graph to the right. $y = 3x + 1$, $y = 3x + 0$, $y = 3x - 1$

What pattern do you notice for the three equations you graphed? How do you explain this pattern? How could you test to see if your explanation is correct?

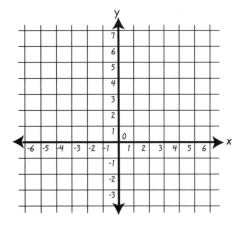

_____

_____

_____

**9.** Try graphing these these equations on the graph to the right: $y = x = 2$, $y = 4x + 2$, $y = -2x + 2$

What patterns do you notice? How do you explain this pattern? How could you test to see if your explanation is correct?

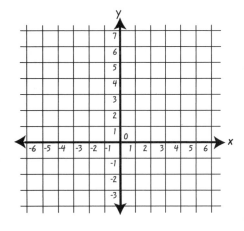

_____

_____

_____

# MORE LINE GRAPHS

Everything weighs less on the moon. That's because the force of gravity is weaker on the moon than it is on Earth. How much would a 100-pound person weigh on the moon?

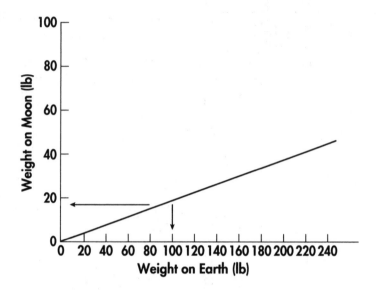

This line graph shows how much something would weigh on the moon. The horizontal axis shows weight in pounds on Earth. The vertical axis shows weight in pounds on the moon. The line that you see on the graph plots the rule for converting earth weight to moon weight.

Look at the arrows on the graph. They show how to line up the data.

Find 100 pounds on the horizontal axis and line up the point on the graph with the vertical axis.

You can see that a 100-pound person would weigh 17 pounds on the moon.

## Guided Practice

1. How much would a 200-pound man weigh on the moon?

   **a.** Find 200 pounds on the horizontal axis.

   **b.** Line up the point on the vertical axis.

   **c.** Write the moon weight. _____

**2.** How much would a rock that weighs 40 pounds on the moon weigh on Earth?

   **a.** Find 40 pounds on the vertical axis.

   **b.** Line up the point on the horizontal axis.

   **c.** Write the Earth weight. _____

## Exercise

The graph shows weights on Mars and Jupiter compared to Earth. A chair that weighs 50 pounds on Earth would weigh:

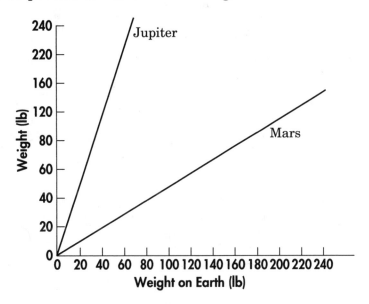

**3.** _____ on Mars.  **4.** _____ on Jupiter.  **5.** _____ on the moon

A rock that weighs 200 pounds on Jupiter would weigh:

**6.** _____ on Earth.  **7.** _____ on Mars.  **8.** _____ on the moon

## Application

**9.** On which planet—Earth, Juniper, or Mars—would things be heaviest? Explain.

_____

_____

**10.** An object weighs 400 pounds on Earth. Estimate how much it would weigh on Mars and Jupiter. Explain how you made your estimate.

_____

_____

# INTERPRETING GRAPHS RELATING TIME AND DISTANCE

## *Reminder*

Speed equals distance divided by time.

Wanda is a bicycle messenger for the Warp Speed Delivery Service. On Thursday morning she rode down Broadway and made three deliveries. What was Wanda's average speed from her office to 165th Street?

This graph shows the part of the trip Wanda made to 165th Street. The horizontal axis shows hours. The vertical axis shows distance in miles. Using this kind of graph and a formula, you can find out how fast Wanda was traveling between each of her stops.

Look at the arrows on the close-up of the graph. The arrows indicate that Wanda rode 4 miles in 0.25 hours. This is the information you need to figure out Wanda's bicycle speed to 165th Street.

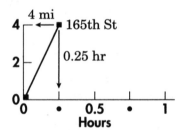

To figure out how fast Wanda was traveling, you can use this formula:

*Average Speed = Distance ÷ Time*

*Average Speed = 4 miles ÷ 0.25 hours*
*= 16 miles per hour*

Wanda's average speed was 16 miles per hour from her office to 165th Street.

At 165th Street, Wanda stopped for 15 minutes. This is shown by the flat line on the graph.

Notice that Wanda's position didn't change for 0.25 hours. She is still 4 miles from her home office.

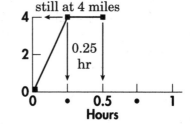

Wanda's average speed during this time period was:

*0 miles ÷ 0.25 hours = 0 miles per hour*

Waiting slowed Wanda down. Her average speed for the whole trip so far was:

$$Average\ Speed = Total\ Distance ÷ Total\ time$$
$$= (4\ mi + 0\ mi) ÷ (0.25\ hr + 0.25\ hr)$$
$$= 4\ mi ÷ 0.5\ hr$$
$$= 8\ miles\ per\ hour$$

After waiting at 165th Street, it took Wanda a half-hour to ride 2 miles to 125th Street.

To draw this on the graph:

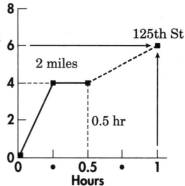

1. Find an additional 0.5 hour on the horizontal axis.

2. Find and additional 2 miles on the vertical scale.

3. Draw a point where the two measurements meet.

4. Draw a line to connect the point to the previous point.

## Guided Practice

From 125th Street, it took Wanda a half-hour to ride 6 miles to 5th Street.

**1.** Draw this part of the trip on the graph above.

    **a.** Find an additional 0.5 hour on the horizontal scale.

    **b.** Find an additional 6 miles on the vertical scale.

    **c.** Draw a line where the two measurements meet.

**2.** What was Wanda's speed from 125th Street to 5th Street?

    **a.** Write the distance she traveled. _____

    **b.** Write the time it took in hours. _____

    **c.** Divide the distance by the time. Write the speed. _____

**3.** What was Wanda's average speed over the entire trip?

    **a.** Write the total distance Wanda traveled. _____

    **b.** Write the total time it took in hours. _____

    **c.** Divide the total distance by the total time. Write the average speed.

_____

## Exercises

Wanda had lunch at 5th Street and Broadway. Then she made three pickups, two of them in Brooklyn. After two of the pickups, she had to wait.

|  | Location | Distance | Time |
|---|---|---|---|
| Pickup 1 | Flatbush Avenue | ? miles | ? minutes |
| STOP 1 |  | ? miles | ? minutes |
| Pickup 2 | Avenue U | 8 miles | 32 minutes |
| STOP 2 |  | 0 miles | 30 minutes |
| Pickup 3 | Canal Street | 10 miles | 45 minutes |

The first two parts of the trip are shown on the graph.

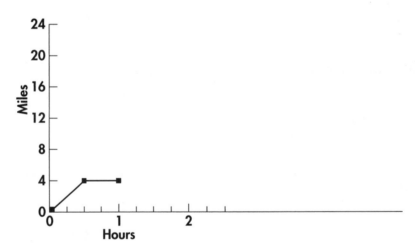

**From the graph, find the:**

    **4.** distance for pickup 1    **5.** time for pickup 1    **6.** distance and time for stop 1

_____    _____    _____

**From the graph, find the speed:**

    **7.** during pickup 1    **8.** during stop 1    **9.** over the whole afternoon trip so far

_____    _____    _____

**On the graph above, graph:**

**10.** Pickup 2          **11.** Stop 2          **12.** Pickup 3

**Find the speed:**

**13.** during pickup 2          **14.** during stop 2          **15.** for the afternoon

_____          _____          _____

**16.** For the whole day, how many total miles did Wanda travel? What was her average speed? _____

## Application

**17.** Chad and Sheila each took a ride in their cars. Chad drove at a steady 40 miles per hour for 3 hours. Sheila drove for an hour at 60 miles per hour, stopped for an hour, then drove another hour at 60 miles per hour. How far did each driver drive?

_____

**18.** Mark followed Chad and Sheila at a speed of 45 miles an hour. How long would it take him to catch up with them?

_____

**19.** Julissa wants to make a 50-mile bike trip. She figures that she'll take two breaks and ride at a steady 15 miles per hour on the trip. How long can her breaks be if she wants to finish the trip in under 3.5 hours?

_____

_____

_____

**20.** Explain how you got your answer to problem 19.

_____

_____

_____

 **SYSTEMS OF LINEAR EQUATIONS**

### Reminder

A linear equation is an equation that can be graphed as a straight line on a coordinate system.

You can make a graph of a linear equation to help solve a problem. If the problem has more than one solution, the graph will show all of them.

**Example:** Two numbers have a sum of 6. What could the numbers be?

Write an equation to describe the problem. Use $x$ and $y$ for the two unknown numbers.

$$x + y = 6$$

Now graph the equation. $x + y = 6$ to visualize all solutions.

| x | y |
|---|---|
| 1 | 5 |
| 4 | 2 |
| 3 | 3 |

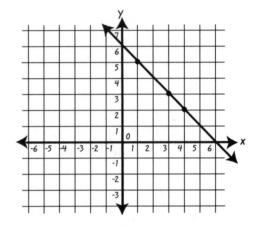

You can see that the line also passes through other points. For example, $(0,6)$, $(2,4)$, $(5,1)$, and $(6,0)$ are solutions. So, the two numbers with a sum of 6 could be 0 and 6, 1 and 5, 2 and 4, or 3 and 3.

Is the pair of numbers 1 and 2 a solution? No, because $(1,2)$ is not on the line. Also, $1 + 2 \neq 6$.

## Guided Practice

1. Olivia has the same birthday as her brother, but she is twice as old. What could their ages be?

   **a.** Let $x$ stand for her brother's age. Let $y$ stand for Olivia's age.

   Then $y =$ _____ $x$

**2.** Graph $y = 2x$

| x | y |
|---|---|
| 3 | 6 |
| **a.** 2 | __ |
| **b.** __ | __ |

**c.** List some ages that Olivia and her brother could be.

_____ and _____

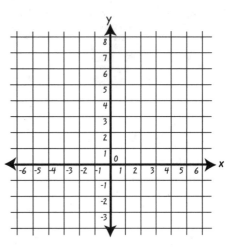

**3.** Two numbers have a sum of 8. What could the numbers be? Write an equation to describe the problem using $x$ and $y$ for the two unknown numbers. Then graph the equation to visualize all the solutions.

| x | y |
|---|---|
| __ | __ |
| __ | __ |
| __ | __ |
| __ | __ |

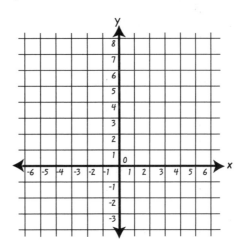

**4.** Inera is 5 years more than twice her sister's age. Could Inera be 27? Could she be 28? Explain. [Hint: Use the equation $y = 2x + 5$ to graph ordered pairs that could be their ages.]

_____

_____

_____

_____

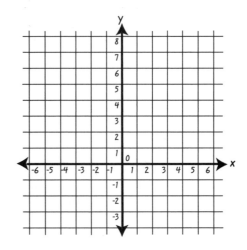

# SOLVING SYSTEMS OF LINEAR EQUATIONS

## Vocabulary

**system of equations:** a pair of equations that is used to solve a problem

Sometimes you can write two equations to help you solve a problem. The numbers that can make *both* equations true are the solution to the problem. The pair of equations that you use is called a **system of equations**.

Example: Two numbers have a sum of 11. One of the numbers is 3 more than the other. What are the numbers?

Using $x$ and $y$ for the two numbers, you can write two equations for the problem.

$$x + y = 11 \quad and \quad x + 3 = y$$

Graph solutions (ordered pairs) of one equation.

$x + y = 11$

| x | y |
|---|---|
| 10 | 1 |
| 7 | 4 |
| 3 | 8 |

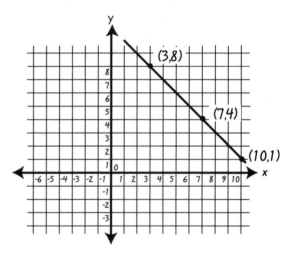

Graph solutions (ordered pairs) of the second equation on the same coordinate grid.

$x + 3 = y$

| x | y |
|---|---|
| 0 | 3 |
| 2 | 5 |

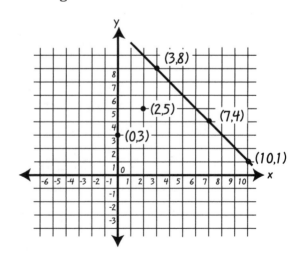

The point where the two lines cross, or intersect, is the solution to both equations and to the problem. The intersection is at (4,7). So $x = 4$ and $y = 7$. The two numbers are 4 and 7.

You can check back to be sure that the solution is correct:

$4 + 7 = 11$, and 7 is 3 more than 4. So the answer is correct.

## Guided Practice

**Solve the system of equations: Equation 1: $y = 2x - 1$**

**Equation 2: $y = {}^-3x + 4$.**

**1.** Find two ordered pairs for Equation 1.

   **a.** Find the value of $y$ when $x = 1$.

   _____

   **b.** Write the ordered pair for $x = 1$.

   _____

   **c.** Find the value of $y$ when $x = 2$.

   _____

   **d.** Write the ordered pair for $x = 2$.

   _____

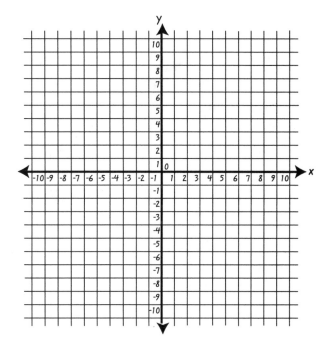

**2.** Find two ordered pairs for Equation 2.

   **a.** Find the value of $y$ when $x = 2$. _____

   **b.** Write the ordered pair for $x = 2$. _____

   **c.** Find the value of $y$ when $x = 1$. _____

   **d.** Write the ordered pair for $x = 1$. _____

**3.** Graph solutions of both equations on the grid above.

   **a.** On the grid, draw each ordered pair you found for Equation 1.

   **b.** Connect the two points for Equation 1.

   **c.** Draw each ordered pair you found for Equation 2.

   **d.** Connect the two points for Equation 2.

**4.** Solve the system of equations.

   **a.** Write the ordered pair for the point where the two lines intersect.

   _____

   **b.** Put values for the intersection point into Equation 1. Does the equation check? _____

   **c.** Put values for the intersection point into Equation 2. Does the equation check? _____

   **d.** What values for $x$ and $y$ solve the system of equations? _____

## Exercises

**5.** Graph a line to show the solutions (ordered pairs) for the equation $y = x - 6$.

**6.** Graph a line to show the solutions (ordered pairs) for the equation $y = {}^-2x + 3$.

**7.** Write the ordered pair that locates where the equations intersect.

   _____

**8.** What is the solution to the system of equations?

   _____

**Use the graph to find the solution for the following problem.**

**9.** Ming is 4 years older than her brother. Their ages add up to 16. How old are they?

   _____

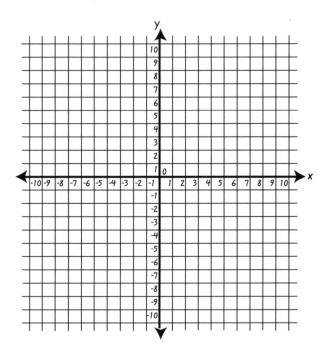

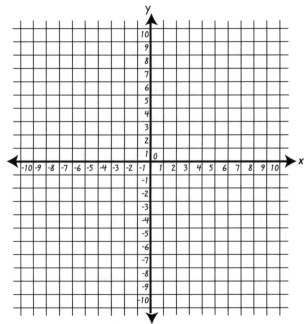

**10.** Make up your own system of equations. Graph the solutions of the equations on the coordinate grid. Find the solution of the system and check it.

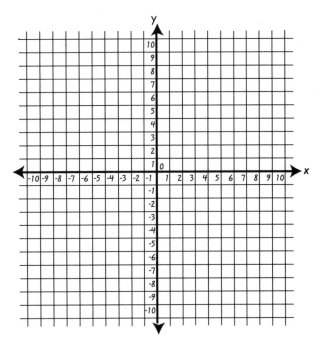

**11.** Graph solutions for the system of equations $y = x + 2$ and $y = x + 3$. Why doesn't this system of equations have a solution? Explain.

_____

_____

_____

**12.** Could a system of linear equations have two solutions? Explain.

_____

_____

_____

# 1-5 CUMULATIVE REVIEW

Lilly bought these gifts for her friends' birthdays this year.

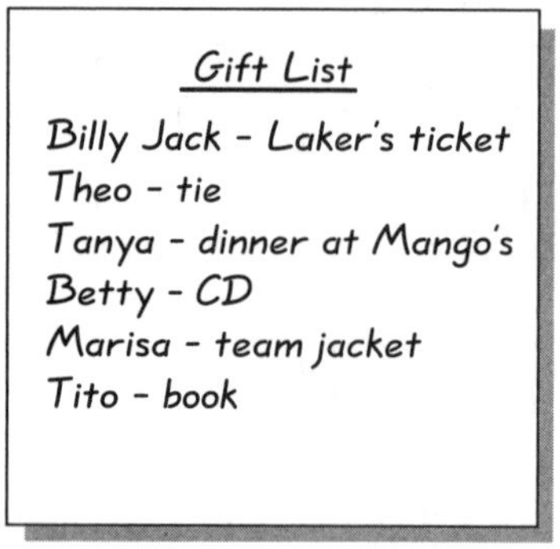

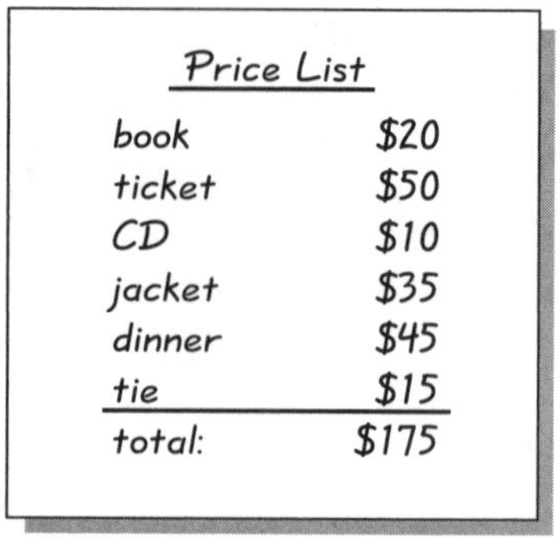

| Gift List | Price List | |
|---|---|---|
| Billy Jack - Laker's ticket | book | $20 |
| Theo - tie | ticket | $50 |
| Tanya - dinner at Mango's | CD | $10 |
| Betty - CD | jacket | $35 |
| Marisa - team jacket | dinner | $45 |
| Tito - book | tie | $15 |
| | total: | $175 |

## Complete the table.

**1.**

| | Book | CD | Tie | Laker ticket | | |
|---|---|---|---|---|---|---|
| **To** | Tito | | Theo | | Marisa | |
| **Price** | $20 | $10 | | | $35 | |

## Name the person to whom Lilly gave each gift.

**2.** Ticket _____  **3.** Tie _____  **4.** Dinner _____

## Write the cost of each gift.

**5.** CD _____  **6.** Jacket _____  **7.** Book

**8.** The graph below shows the price of each gift Lilly bought for her friends last year. Graph the information from the above table to show how much Lilly spent on gifts this year.

**9.** Compare the gift prices for the two years. Whose gift prices increased? Whose decreased? Whose increased the most? Decreased the most?

_____

_____

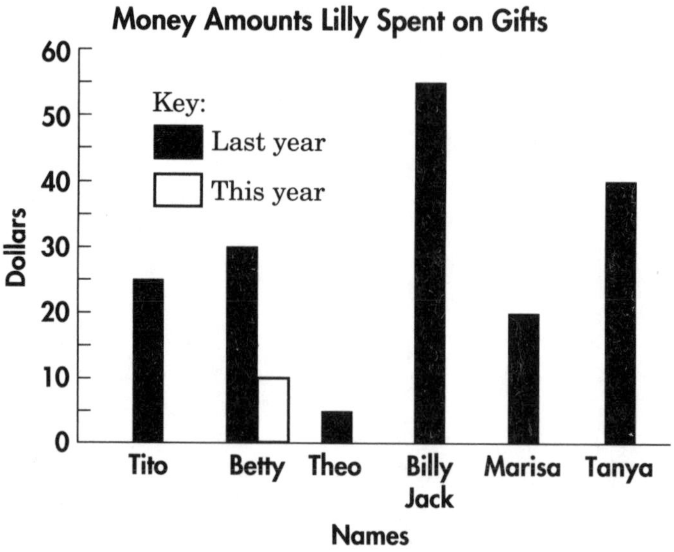

**Money Amounts Lilly Spent on Gifts**

Key:
■ Last year
□ This year

Dollars

Tito  Betty  Theo  Billy Jack  Marisa  Tanya

Names

# 6-10 CUMULATIVE REVIEW

Victor did a survey on how much he and his friends spent on video games.

**Write the amount each person spent on video games.**

**1.** Victor _____

**2.** Gabriela _____

**3.** Kalil _____

**Money Spent on Video Games**

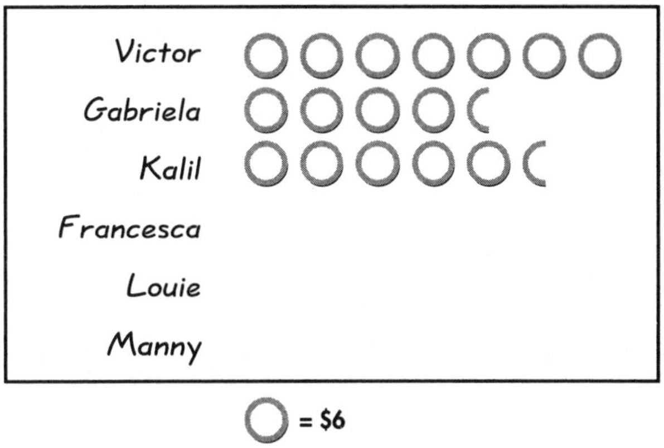

| | |
|---|---|
| Victor | ○○○○○○ |
| Gabriela | ○○○○( |
| Kalil | ○○○○○( |
| Francesca | |
| Louie | |
| Manny | |

○ = $6

**Replace the money amounts with symbols on the pictograph for these players.**

**4.** Francesca ($48)    **5.** Louie ($21)    **6.** Manny ($39)

**Write the amount that Victor spent on video games during each month.**

**7.** February _____

**8.** April _____

**9.** May _____

**Victor's Monthly Video Game Expenses**

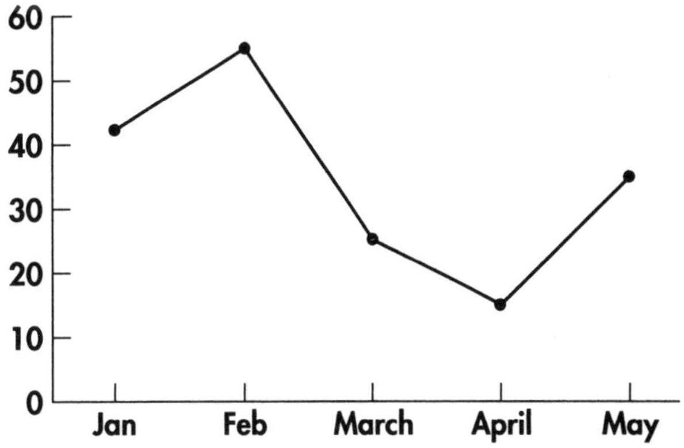

**During which month did Victor spend:**

**10.** the least _____

**11.** the most _____

**12.** The table below shows the amount Gabriela spent on video games. Graph the data on the graph above to make a double-line graph and then analyze your findings.

| Month | Jan. | Feb. | Mar. | Apr. | May |
|---|---|---|---|---|---|
| Amount | $27 | $44 | $20 | $20 | $30 |

# 11-13 CUMULATIVE REVIEW

The circle graph shows the largest eyewear stores in the United States.

**Write the company that sold the:**

**Eyewear Sales in 1994**

1. most _____

2. least _____

3. second most _____

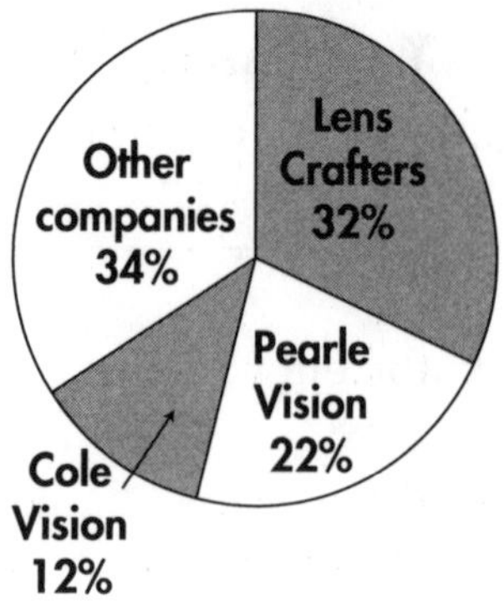

**What is the angle for each part of the circle graph?**

4. Pearle Vision _____

5. Other companies _____

6. Cole Vision _____

At Pearle Vision, 80% of the customers buy metal frames, 5% buy plastic frames, and 15% buy contact lenses.

**Write these percentages as parts of a circle in degrees.**

7. metal frames _____

8. plastic frames _____

9. contact lenses _____

10. Use a protractor to graph the Pearle Vision data.

**Pearle Vision Sales**

11. What fraction of customers buys eyewear from one of the big three eyewear makers?

   Estimate. _____

12. What fraction of all eyewear customers buys metal frames from Pearle Vision? Explain how you got your estimate.

   _____

   _____

Rennie made a histogram to show how many minutes late the bus was over a three-week period.

**Write the number of times the bus was:**

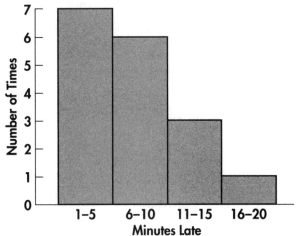

Number of Times

7
6
5
4
3
2
1
0

1–5    6–10    11–15    16–20

Minutes Late

**1.** 1 to 5 minutes late _____

**2.** 6 to 10 minutes late _____

**3.** 11 to 15 minutes late _____

**4.** How many bus trips are shown on the histogram? _____

**5.** How many times was the bus on time during this time? _____

**6.** Analyze the histogram. What patterns do you see?

_____

The table shows how many books Lydia took out of the library for a period of 11 weeks.

| Week | 1 | 2 | 3 | 4 | 5 | 6 | 7 | 8 | 9 | 10 | 11 |
|------|----|---|---|----|----|---|----|---|---|----|----|
| Books | 16 | 8 | 4 | 14 | 20 | 8 | 10 | 6 | 8 | 3 | 3 |

**7.** range _____    **8.** median _____    **9.** mode _____

 **10.** Find the total number of books Lydia took out of the library. Use this total to find the mean number of books that she took out.

_____

**11.** Lydia claims that she reads about 1,000 books per year. Do you think that she is right? _____

Roberta worked 7 days in a row delivering pizzas. These are the amounts of money she made each day:  $12, $18, $15, $24, $21, $30, $36

**1.** Graph the above data on this stem-and-leaf plot.

**Dollars Roberta Made**

How many days did Roberta make:

**2.** less than $20?

**3.** more than $30?

**4.** more than $20?

_____

_____

_____

**5.** Roberta worked two more days: she made $14 on Monday and $19 dollars on Tuesday. Show this new data on the stem-and-leaf plot.

**6.** By looking at the stem-and-leaf plot, what could you say is an average

amount of money that Roberta makes each day? _____

Roberta collected this data about the number of hours she worked and how much she made in a week: 2 hours-$12, 2.5 hours-$15, 3 hours-$18, 3.5 hours-$21, 4 hours-$24, 5 hours-$30, 6 hours-$36.

**Make a scattergram to show the two sets of data. Each point represents a money amount.**

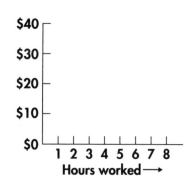

**7.** Does the scattergram above show correlation? How do you know? What kind of correlation does it show? What does this correlation mean?

_____

_____

_____

The graph shows Sammy's weight gain using Muscle Power sports drink.

**1.** Sammy started using Muscle Power in February. What effect did it seem to have on Sammy's weight?

_____

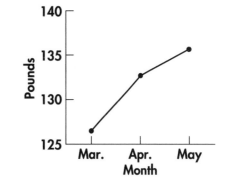

**2.** How many pounds did Sammy lose or gain using Muscle Power? _____

The table below shows Sammy's weight over a longer period of time.

| Month | Jan. | Feb. | Mar. | Apr. | May | Jun. | Jul. | Aug. |
|--------|------|------|------|------|-----|------|------|------|
| Weight | 128 | 130 | 126 | 133 | 136 | 134 | 131 | 128 |

How much did Sammy weigh:

**3.** when he started using Muscle Power? _____

**4.** when he stopped using Muscle Power in August? _____

**5.** Over the entire time he used Muscle Power, how many pounds did Sammy gain or lose? _____

**6.** What was misleading about the above graph? Explain.

_____

All 12 members of Sammy's weight training class took Muscle Power for 3 months. This graph shows the results.

**7.** By the end of 3 months, how many pounds did the entire class gain?

_____

**8.** What was the average weight gain for a typical member of the class?

_____

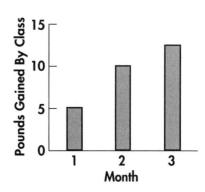

**1.** Write the *x*-value for this ordered pair: (1,4) _____

**2.** Write the *y*-value for this ordered pair: (2,⁻3) _____

**3.** Graph the ordered pairs from problems 1 and 2 below.

**Write the ordered pair that
gives the location of:**

**4.** Point A _____

**5.** Point B _____

**6.** Point C _____

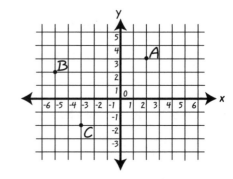

**For the equation *y* = 2*x* - 3, write the value of *y* when:**

**7.** *x* = 2                          **8.**  *x* = 1

_____                          _____

**9.** Write the ordered pairs from problems 7 and 8. _____

   **a.** Graph the two ordered pairs on the above coordinate grid.

   **b.** Draw a line through the points you made.

**10.** This graph shows mileage and time
for Roberta's first pizza delivery.
On this delivery, Roberta traveled:

   **a.** how many miles? _____

   **b.** in how long? _____

   **c.** at what average speed? _____

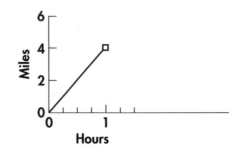

**11.** Roberta waited for 30 minutes after her first delivery. then it took her
15 minutes to go 2 miles for her second delivery. Show these two events
on the graph.

**12.** What was Roberta's total distance and time for both deliveries? What
was her average speed for both deliveries?

# CUMULATIVE REVIEW

**1.** Two numbers have the same sum of 10. What could the numbers be? Write an equation to describe the problem using $x$ and $y$ for the two unknown numbers. Then graph the equation to visualize all the solutions.

| **x** | **y** |
|---|---|
| ___ | ___ |
| ___ | ___ |
| ___ | ___ |

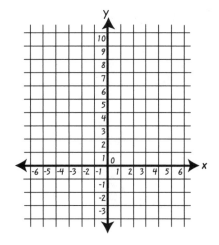

**2.** Use a graph to solve this system of equations:

Equation 1          Equation 2
$y = 2x + 5$          $y = -2x + 1$

**a.** Graph Equation 1.

**b.** Graph Equation 2.

**c.** Identify the ordered pair where the two equations intersect. What are the values for $x$ and $y$?

_____

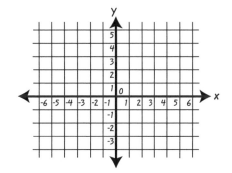

**d.** Check your answer by using the values you found for both $x$ and $y$ in Equation 2. Show each step.

**3.** Solve this system of three equations by graphing: $y = x$, $y = {}^-x + 4$, $y = 2x - 2$. At what point do all three equations intersect?

_____

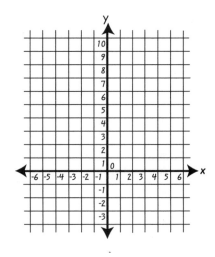

# ANSWER KEY

**LESSON 1** (pages 2–3)
 **1. a.** fifth, or last **b.** third **c.** 2,078
 **3. a.** 24 **b.** 26 **c.** 56
 **5.** Wednesday, Tuesday
 **7.** Peg showed steady improvement. Anton was steady, but didn't improve. Sheray was strong but erratic.

**LESSON 2** (pages 4–5)
 **1. a.** 1.4, 2.9 **b.** 4.3 **c.** See students' tables.
 **d.** 6.2
 **3.** Row 1: 3, 1, 2, 4. Row 2: Ocean Princess, King Lou, Sea Breeze, Billy-Bob. Row 3: 605, 520, 409, 395
 **5.** Answers may vary.

**LESSON 3** (pages 6–7)
 **1. a.** 38,000 **b.** 20,000 **c.** 18,000
 **3.** 60,000
 **5.** 90,000
 **7.** 260,000
 **9.** Alaska, Washington, North Carolina, Texas, New York, Michigan

**LESSON 4** (pages 8–9)
 **1. a.** 72
 **3.** See students' graphs.
 **5.** Answers will vary.

**LESSON 5** (pages 10–11)
 **1. a.** 14 **b.** 5 **c.** 4
 **3.** Wheaties
 **5.** 3, 3
 **7.** Answers may vary.

**LESSON 6** (pages 12–13)
 **1. a.** 6 **b.** $6 \times 80 + 0 \times 40$ **c.** 480
 **3.** cheese
 **5.** pepperoni
 **7.** 170
 **9.** cheese: about $1,700, pepperoni: about $1,200, mushroom: about $300, other: about $800
 **11.** $208,000

**LESSON 7** (pages 14–15)
 **1. a.** 2
 **3. a.** 4
 **5.** Students should justify choice of symbol and amount it represents.

**LESSON 8** (pages 16–17)
 **1. c.** about 183 lb
 **3. a.** about 180 lb **b.** about 180 lb **c.** 195 lb
 **5. a.** 5th month **b.** 2nd month **c.** 6th month

**LESSON 9** (pages 18–19)
 **1. a.** 26
 **3.** See students' graphs.

**LESSON 10** (pages 20–21)
 **1. a.** rock **b.** 65,000 **c.** 38,000
 **3.** See students' graphs.
 **5.** Rock: Week 2, Rap: Week 5
 **7.** Week 3
 **9.** Between Weeks 5 and 6
 **11.** Answers may vary.

**LESSON 11** (pages 22–23)
 **1. a.** video **b.** $1,600 million **c.** 72%
 **3.** theater movies
 **5.** 80% inside, 20% outside
 **7.** Answers will vary.

**LESSON 12** (pages 24–25)
 **1. c.** 60 degrees
 **3.** 80 degrees
 **5.** 40 degrees
 **7.** 90 degrees represents each of the other two movies

**LESSON 13** (pages 26–27)
 **1. a.** 4.9 million **b.** 62% **c.** 223 degrees
 **3.** See students' graphs.

**LESSON 14** (pages 28–29)
 **1. a.** 7.0–7.975 **b.** 1 time
 **3.** 61–70 inches
 **5.** 71–75 inches
 **7.** Answers may vary. Students should see a general bell-shaped curve, with the most people in the center portion of the histogram.

**LESSON 15** (pages 30–31)
 **1. a.** 11 **b.** 50 **c.** 6.25
 **3.** 36
 **5.** $425
 **7.** $136
 **9.** Roy had many more tickets and fines than the others. He pushed the average to a much higher level than it otherwise would have been.

**LESSON 16** (pages 32–33)
　**1. b.** 19
　**3.** 7
　**5.** 11
　**7.** 6
　**9.** 9.9
　**11.** 14.1
　**13.** Answers may vary. The mean is over 1 million dollars, but this is pushed up by a few very high salaries. The median gives a view of where the center of the whole distribution of salaries lies.

**LESSON 17** (pages 34–35)
　**1. a.** 4  **b.** 7
　**3.** 3
　**5.** 10
　**7.** 4
　**9. a.** Answers may vary. Typical scores are either about 100 or about 165. In other words, the distribution is bimodal.
　**b.** Answers will vary, but perhaps they should create two leagues—one for low scorers and one for high scorers.

**LESSON 18** (pages 36–39)
　**1. a.** 2  **b.** $70  **c.** ticket 3
　**3.** $56
　**5.** 6
　**7.** 48
　**9.** horizontal
　**11.** See students' graphs.
　**13.** Students will probably predict a positive correlation.

**LESSON 19** (pages 40–43)
　**1. a.** Diamond  **b.** about 3 times as large
　**c.** about $1.50
　**3. a.** 2%  **b.** 88%  **c.** 1 or 2 persons
　**5.** less
　**7.** 20
　**9.** 4%
　**11.** increasing
　**13.** decreasing
　**15.** August
　**17.** They left out several months. They showed only the months in which new customers increased. They presented the data this way to make it look like business was increasing rather than decreasing.

**LESSON 20** (pages 44–45)
　**1. a.** Utah  **b.** 4 more  **c.** 0
　**3.** Houston, Denver
　**5.** Denver, Dallas, Minnesota
　**7.** Denver

　**9.** 9
　**11.** Utah will have more wins, 50 to 49, but San Antonio will have fewer losses, 21 to 18. Games behind says that San Antonio would be in first place. A calculator shows that winning percentages would be: San Antionio: .732, Utah: .704, putting San Antonio in first place. To calculate the winning percentage for a team, divide the games won by the games played.

**LESSON 21** (pages 46–47)
　**1. a.** 250  **b.** $625  **c.** $425
　**3.** 320
　**5.** $280
　**7.** $200
　**9.** Week 10: $437.50 and Week 5: $425

**LESSON 22** (pages 48–49)
　**1. a.** 3  **b.** 4  **c.** (3,4)
　**3.** ($^-$1,2)
　**5.** ($^-$2,$^-$2)
　**7.** See students' graphs.
　**9.** a house
　**11.** Sample answer: (1, 2) and (2, 1); Other answers are possible.

**LESSON 23** (pages 50–53)
　**1. b.** $x = 3, y = 7$  **c.** (3, 7)
　**3. b.** $x = {}^-1, y = 3$
　**5. a.** 3  **b.** 1  **c.** $^-$2  **d.** (8,3), (6,1), (3,$^-$2)
　**7.** All 3 equations are parallel. Students may notice that the only thing that changed was the $y$-intercept number — in these 3 equations it changed from 2 to 1 to 0. If students recognized that this changed the location of the line, they may have thought to test their hypothesis by trying an equation like $y = 3x + 4$ to see if it was parallel.

**LESSON 24** (pages 54–55)
　**1. c.** 34 lb
　**3.** 19 lb
　**5.** 9 lb
　**7.** 29 lb
　**9.** On Jupiter things would be heaviest, because, as problems 6–8 show, something that weighs 200 lb on Jupiter would weigh less on Earth, Mars, and the moon.

**LESSON 25** (pages 56–59)
　**1.** See students' graphs.
　**3. a.** 12 miles  **b.** 1.5 hours  **c.** 8 mph
　**5.** 30 minutes
　**7.** 12 mph
　**9.** 4 mph

**11.** See students' graphs.

**13.** 15 mph

**15.** 8.3 mph

**17.** They both drove 120 miles.

**19.** She can take two 5-minute breaks. Other solutions that add up to 10 minutes are also possible, such as one 6-minute break and one 4-minute break, 7 and 3, 8 and 2, etc.

**LESSON 26** (pages 60–61)

**1. a.** 2

**3.** Answers will vary.

**LESSON 27** (pages 62–65)

**1. a.** 1 **b.** (1, 1) **c.** 3 **d.** (2, 3)

**3.** See students' graphs.

**5.** See students' graphs.

**7.** (3, ⁻3)

**9.** Ming is 10; her brother is 6.

**11.** The two lines are parallel. They don't intersect so they don't have a solution.

**CUMULATIVE REVIEW: LESSONS 1–5** (page 66)

**1.** See students' tables.

**3.** Theo

**5.** $10

**7.** $20

**9.** Increased: Theo, Marissa, Tanya; decreased: Tito, Betty, Billy Jack; increased the most: Marissa, decreased the most: Betty

**CUMULATIVE REVIEW: LESSONS 6–10** (page 67)

**1.** $42

**3.** $33

**5.** 3.5 coins

**7.** $55

**9.** $35

**11.** February

**CUMULATIVE REVIEW: LESSONS 11–13** (page 68)

**1.** Lens Crafters

**3.** Pearle Vision

**5.** 122 degrees

**7.** 288 degrees

**9.** 18 degrees

**11.** about $\frac{2}{3}$

**CUMULATIVE REVIEW: LESSONS 14–16** (page 69)

**1.** 7

**3.** 3

**5.** 0

**7.** 17

**9.** 8

**11.** Answers will vary.

**CUMULATIVE REVIEW: LESSONS 17–20** (page 70)

**1.** See students' graphs.

**3.** 1

**5.** See students' graphs.

**7.** It shows a positive correlation because both sets of data increase. This correlation means that the hours Roberta worked are directly related to the amount of money she made. NOTE: On the scattergram above, you could show a little less than perfect correlation; e.g., Roberta could work 5 hours and make $32 instead of exactly $30.

**CUMULATIVE REVIEW: LESSONS 21–23** (page 71)

**1.** gained

**3.** 130

**5.** He lost 2 pounds.

**7.** about 12 pounds

**CUMULATIVE REVIEW: LESSONS 22–25** (page 72)

**1.** 1

**3.** See students' graphs.

**5.** (⁻3,3)

**7.** 1

**9.** (⁻2,1), (1,⁻1)

**11.** See students' graphs.

**CUMULATIVE REVIEW: LESSONS 26–27** (page 73)

**1.** Answers will vary.

**3.** They intersect at (2,2) or $x = 2$, $y = 2$